LEVEL UP

Gaining Power During the Fight

Dr. Latoshia Daniels

DEDICATION

*To everyone who is determined to overcome difficulties
and be bold enough to embrace the process of healing...
this one is for us.*

ACKNOWLEDGMENT

I want to give a special thank you to my amazing husband. You entered the storm with me and never backed down. You saw me for who I am and not my situation. Not once did you judge me. You are my safe place, and I am grateful that God willed you to me. Thank you for being obedient to our Father. I love you to the third heaven and back. Thank you for a beautiful level-three relationship.

To my fellas. You two are amazing and I am proud to be your mother. I am grateful for the gifts God gave me in each one of you. Thank you for loving me unconditionally and for forgiving me for causing you pain. Thank you for the encouraging words and prayers. Ma loves you.

To my support system during this GAP season. Each of you has been my anchor and did not lose faith but instead used your faith to aid me with remaining kingdom focused in this season of pain and suffering and transformation. Thank you for adding value to my life. I love you.

To my beloved firstborn. You are not here to read this, but I want to acknowledge that you may be gone but you will never be forgotten. You live forever in my heart. You are Ma's boy for life.

Table of Contents

Dedication   3

Acknowledgment   4

About the Author   6

Introduction   9

Chapter One : Opponent   13

Chapter Two: The Strategy   25

Chapter Three: Recognize   33

Chapter Four: Reconcile   45

Chapter Five: Rededicate   58

Chapter Six: Relinquish   68

Chapter Seven: Reclaim   83

Chapter Eight:: Refine   95

Chapter Nine: Release   104

Conclusion   121

ABOUT THE AUTHOR

Dr. Latoshia Daniels is a wife and mother first but is willing to do all she can to aid others in becoming the best they can be. She is the founder of Links of Love (L.O.L.), a nonprofit that aims to empower and mentor youth and young adults. She is a graduate of Walden University, where she received a Doctor of Social Work degree. She obtained her Master of Social Work from the University of Arkansas at Little Rock. Dr. Daniels has an intentional agenda of combining the Word of God with her clinical knowledge in mental and behavioral health to help others to heal from emotional wounds and be placed in a position where they will be able to receive all God has for them. She gives God all the glory for the favor that is upon her life.

"I do not capitalize the name satan or related names because I choose not to acknowledge him, even to the point of violating grammatical rules."

INTRODUCTION

"Blessed is the man who endures temptation; for when he has been approved, he will receive the crown of life which the Lord has promised to those who love Him."
- James 1:12 NKJV

Have you ever been, or are you currently in the fight of your life? I am. Life has planted many powerful blows that changed the trajectory of my life. Amid this fight, I gained powerful insight that kept me standing and pressing forward, believing God has more for my life. That my life is not over but just beginning.

My middle son, Dre, and I became intentional about discussing God's Word weekly. This decision allowed us to grow in our relationship with God while maintaining our bond amidst a disruption in life. During one of our scheduled times to discuss the Word, Dre, 21 years old at the time, was hanging out with his little brother, CJ, my baby boy age 10 years old. I absolutely love their bond, and I am grateful for it. I began the discussion on James 1:12 after prayer. Once I shared the insight I gained and Dre shared his thoughts, I asked CJ if he had any input. I assured him it was okay if he did not since he was not prepared. His reply was, "I do." He proceeded to share his insight using the analogy of playing his video game. "Mom, it's like when I am on my game, and I am weaker than my opponent. I have to level up so I can defeat him." Dre summarized the discussion by saying, "My queen, it is round 12. You have to keep fighting until the final bell sounds." My baby added, "And level up, mom."

I learned a valuable lesson from my fellas on that inspiring day. Never doubt what you can learn from your children. I was so encouraged that I asked them jokingly, "Who is your mother?" She must be so proud of you two." They both stated boldly, "You!" Come on, Jesus! I am truly blessed and grateful.

To give you a little background on why this discussion with my fellas was so significant for me, no for us. I was incarcerated at the time of having the conversation with them. I was waiting for my day in court. At the time of the conversation, I had been away from my children for three years. At this point, my children experienced significant loss, and so did I. My absence from their daily lives, the death of their oldest brother, and our home and many materials- sentimental things. Life as they knew it was destroyed, and they lacked the reason for why. However, they still maintained joy, peace, and hope. They still love me and have hope of God reuniting us. The boys often provided me with words of encouragement to keep me kingdom-focused. Their words of encouragement set the tone for Level Up.

In my quest to level up, I became more intentional about fussing, pushing, and pressing. When I say that, I mean I began…

1. To F.U.S.S. (Faith Until Something Shakes) harder.

2. To P.U.S.H. (Pray Until Something Happens) more.

3. To P.R.E.S.S. (Pray Releasing Every Stressful Situation).

Such determination established my "faith attitude" as I waited patiently with and on the Lord to release me from the "G.A.P." - (God Allowed Pause). I call this season my "GAP" because I was stagnant and isolated as God did a great work in me. There are many things I failed to understand, but I accepted that God allowed it. The pause was necessary because I had strayed from the beacon path. A detour was needed to get my attention and place me back in alignment with God's will and plan for my life. This "GAP" has given me the time to recognize what I was missing and why I made the choices I made. I have been able to heal spiritually, mentally, and emotionally from my past and embrace the healed me, the woman whom God designed me to be.

As I pondered on the message my fellas impressed upon me on that day of discussing James 1:12, I sought the Lord for clarity and understanding. I understood that my fight was not physical. Spiritual warfare is real, and it has a direct impact on the natural world. Christians such as I must understand this fact and learn to fight with the right weapons and fight the right enemy. Thinking about CJ's advice, I sought the Lord to give me true wisdom and knowledge about my enemy and how to level up over my opponent.

This book is my testament to how I learned to gain strength during this challenging season. I learned to have freedom under difficult circumstances through my broken surrender and coming to full agreement with God. To gain strength from the trials and be loosed from strongholds that bound me. I gained an understanding of what I viewed as a hindrance, in essence, allowed me to be strengthened in character. I leveled up in strength from applying faith to patiently face life's problems. Knowing the true enemy and using God's Word to stand against opposition. I've learned to fight the good fight of faith and to be renewed daily in my mind. Such renewal develops and maintains what is necessary to survive and preserve during trials and tribulations beyond understanding. The renewal aided me in maintaining and preserving during the judicial process as I waited to regain physical freedom.

You may also be in a fight to overcome some form of bondage-physical, mental, emotional, spiritual, or financial. I encourage you to recognize and accept that it's round 12. It's not time to give up but to level up. Instead of succumbing to pain, despair, depression, doubt, loss, confusion, confinement, lack, and more, choose to level up. To apply faith, release love, and rise above it all to defeat that which was set to take you out. I had to be loosed from those things that had me

bound. Things that weighed me down. By doing so, I gained strength. Such strength kept me as I patiently endured my troubles. It sustained me as I waited for the final bell to sound and end the round-season. Proper application of faith and love can do the same for you in your season of trouble. It is time to come out of the corner and get off the ropes. You may feel stuck and pinned down by your problems. Life may be throwing some mighty blows. I am encouraging you to hold your hands up and do not throw in the towel. Look out your eyes of faith. You will see an opportunity to throw the right combination for the knockout (KO). That final jab-jab-cross to receive the V.I.C.T.O.R.Y. Remember, God has the final say. Keep fighting until the final bell sounds. As the songwriter Maurette Brown Clark stated, "It ain't over until God says it's over. Keep fighting until your victory is won."

CHAPTER ONE

OPPONENT

In every battle or fight, there is an enemy. The enemy is the devil for Christians who are committed to fulfilling God's plan. Many of us fail to recognize the true enemy and turn our focus on the person who has harmed us or caused us some form of pain. We seek to attack flesh and blood. As believers, we must recognize and accept that the devil is our true enemy. He is sneaky, and he will try to use any and everything to take us out. He will do whatever he can to keep us from leveling up over him – gaining new ground. The enemy does not fight fair. We not only stand against him, but we also stand against his imps, wiles, tricks, schemes, and deceit – his shenanigans.

KNOW THY ENEMY

Many believers fall short of God's glory by continually falling into the enemy's traps because we lack truth about our "true" enemy and his means of operation. Instead of doing our research, we listen to others and only get partial information. Many need to understand that the devil is slick and has an arsenal of weapons that he uses. We become so busy looking at the troubles that we fail to see and avoid his tactics. After reading this chapter, I pray you will know your "true" enemy and no longer fall prey to his manipulation and lies. No more being tricked out of our spots. Christians call satan many things, including – the devil, Lucifer, the wicked one, the enemy, the serpent, the liar, the snake, the evil one, the tempter, the trickster, and more. My question is, do we know him despite all the names we call him? If you answer yes, you can help me write this chapter because we need all the help we can get. All believers, members of Team Jesus, require knowledge of who the "true enemy" is and how to resist him and not fall prey to his evil ways.

My knowledge of who the enemy of my soul is comes from God's Word and life experiences. I wish I could have learned what I needed from the Word alone to avoid the tough lessons and pain that came with experience. Nonetheless, I have both biblical and practical knowledge. I will share both with the hope of helping you gain the necessary knowledge or confirm, grow, and strengthen your understanding of the "true enemy." The aim is to keep the family of believers from being tricked out of our spots again. No more being manipulated, used, and defeated by or succumbing to the devil's evil ways. I encourage you not to give the devil more power than he has.

The Enemy Is

Satan means "the adversary," he seeks to ensure we have a wrong understanding of God's character.

The thief - John 10:10.

A roaring lion - I Peter 5:8 (CEV).

An angel of light - 2 Corinthians 11:14.

The devil - John 8:44.

A liar - John 8:44.

The accuser– Revelation 12:10.

Lucifer – Isaiah 14:12.

The serpent- Genesis 3:1a.

As we can see, my friends, the enemy, have many names. All of which is an indication of his character. Just as he showed up in the Old Testament and Jesus' days, he continues showing himself in the same manner.

The adversary, the opposer, however, we identify him, is not our friend. He is called many things because he does too much. Come on, think about it. Anyone who gets kicked out of heaven has some severe issues. Where they do that at? I'm trying to get to heaven and stay there.

Satan became God's enemy when he disobeyed our Father. He thought he had the power to overthrow Abba. Michael and the other angels were not going. So, the fight was on. They won (of course), and the devil lost (as to be expected). No one will ever be greater and mightier than our Father. Revelations 12 provides the details for the fall of satan.

So, we have this evil spirit, angel, dragon, serpent, or demon thing out to get us. Why? Because he is trying to save himself. He knows we are a threat to him, and the evil angels kicked out of heaven with him. He wants to keep us from fully knowing who our Father is, who we are, and the purpose God has placed in us. He does not want us to understand and be strengthened by the power in us through our fellowship with Christ.

His name tells us what he desires to do to us. The following names are ones I have identified that we must be aware of in our times of trouble. We associate the devil with our problems but need to gain knowledge of how he gains access. His names identify his character. His nature. They reveal his motives and goals toward us.

He is a thief and a murderer. He wants to steal our hope, kill our dreams, and destroy our lives. Anything and everything that keeps us connected to Christ, he sets out to steal, kill, and destroy. He will do all he can to gain access to our lives. He will go as far as to steal our faith and hope so that we will lose trust in our Creator. Once faith and hope are gone, he can quickly destroy our relationship with Christ. Once we stray from our divine protection, he leaves us in the world to die – spiritually and potentially physically especially if we engage in behaviors detrimental to our health and overall well-being. Bottom-line, the enemy wants access to your life to steal God's Word from you, which kills your power and destroys lives here on earth and eternally.

How does he operate?

The devil is an influencer and very cunning. He uses his charisma to rally followers. Think about it; he did get other angels to engage in his shenanigans in heaven. Then poor Eve was no match for this master manipulator. Operating on a psychological and spiritual level, the devil employs various tactics to tempt and deceive individuals. One of the primary methods used by the devil is to exploit human weaknesses and desires. By appealing to our innate vulnerabilities, greed, pride, or lust, the devil presents enticing offers or opportunities that promise immediate gratification or power. These temptations often come disguised as harmless or desirable choices, subtly leading individuals away from the path of righteousness and towards a darker, self-centered existence.

Greed-covetousness: 1 Timothy 6:10

Lust-sensuality: James 1:13-15

Another way the devil operates is by exploiting doubts and insecurities within individuals. The devil preys upon our fears, uncertainties, and feelings of inadequacy, whispering destructive thoughts and planting seeds of doubt. By undermining our faith, the devil seeks to wear away our trust in God and manipulate us into turning away from the light. The devil's methods can be subtle, gradually eroding our moral compass and convincing us to indulge in destructive behaviors or embrace a worldview that opposes goodness and love. Ultimately, the devil's goal separates us from our connection to our divine Father, leaving our souls vulnerable to darkness and despair.

Affliction – persecution: 2 Timothy 3:12

Anxiety – woes of the world: Philippians 4:6

The enemy has the power of suggestion. He receives power from us once he can gain access to our thoughts. He is very clever and smooth. He will take the truth and change one word or pose (ask) it to you in a way that causes you to doubt what you know. He will tell a lethal lie and dash it with a bit of truth which equates to deception and cause our downfall. Let's travel back to the beginning with the situation with Adam and Eve, but Eve in particular – Genesis 3.

> *"Now the serpent was more cunning than any beast of the field which the Lord God had made. And he said to the woman, "Has God indeed said,' you shall not eat of every tree of the garden'?" (Genesis 3:1.)*

Do you see the question he posed to Eve? It has truth but watch Eve's response and how things change afterward. Mind you; the serpent asked this question as if it was innocent and out of concern.

> *And the woman said to the serpent, "We may eat the fruit of the trees of the garden; but of the fruit of the tree which is in the midst of the garden God has said, 'You shall not eat it, nor shall you touch it, lest you die.'*
> *- Genesis 3:2-3.)*

Do you see where Eve set herself up for failure? She misquoted God, giving the clever one access to do what he is about to do next. Before we move on, let me remind you of God's command to Adam.

> *"And the Lord God commanded the man saying, Of every tree of the garden you may freely eat; but of the tree of the knowledge of good and evil you shall not eat, for in the day that you eat of it you shall surely die."*
> *– Genesis 2:16-17.*

Let's keep going. We see that Eve gave the serpent access with her response. Now watch how he takes quick advantage of the opportunity.

*Then the serpent said to the woman, "You will not surely
die. For God knows your eyes will be open, and you will
be like God, knowing good and evil". -Genesis 3:4.*

Do you see that? He used her words against her while still speaking
what was true. She said by touching the tree; she would die. The evil
one knew she wouldn't because that is not what God said. He already
knew what God said before he approached her in verse one. Then he
went on to speak more truth, but in a way to deceive Eve. To get her
pumped up to take action. Now check out what happens next.

*So when the woman saw that the tree was good for food,
pleasant to the eyes, and desirable to make one wise, she
ate its fruit. She also gave it to her husband
with her, and he ate it. (v6)*

This is getting good! Now we all know that Eve had looked upon
that tree many times. Suddenly, it appeals to her sight after talking to
the evil one. It looks good enough to eat now that she's stared at it.
It has become a desire. How many times have you seen someone and
never had any form of physical attraction to them? Then one day,
out of the blue, when you are vulnerable, the person speaks to you,
approaches you, and now that person is the sexiest thang in the world.
You have acquired a taste for that person. Has anyone been in this
situation? Pick me. I have been there, done that so I can understand
what happened to Eve. The enemy can manipulate us, so what was
once off-limits spiritually and morally is now fair game.

Check out the rest of the verse. After Eve took (touched) and
ate from the tree, she turned around and gave some to Adam. You
see, the devil will cause you to bring down those around you if you
are not careful. He is out to kill your soul and everyone on the Lord's
side. I would like to believe that Adam walked up on the scene and did
not know all that had transpired before he ate the fruit or when Eve
misquoted God in verse 3. For Adam to be present and not correct,
Eve sheds light on another issue we must be aware of. God gave Adam

the command regarding the forbidden tree, yet he stood silent as Eve misquoted God's instructions. I believe that to keep Eve happy, Adam did not speak up, leading to disobedience. My friends, there are times when our loved ones may see satan's influence on us, and they stand by without saying anything and watch us make a self-destructive decision that eventually has an adverse impact on them as well as us.

Look at what happens next.

Then the eyes of both of them were opened, and they knew they were naked; they sewed fig leaves together and made themselves coverings (v7).

The devil had completed his goal once Adam and Eve allowed him to trick them and cause them to go against God. He left them without covering like he does all who fall for his deception. The devil will trap and take us away from our safe place with God so that we will be naked, afraid, and desperate. He leaves us to have to answer to God alone in our mess.

Much like Adam and Eve, we hide (try to hide) from God because we fear the consequences of our disobedience. The exposure leaves us confused because we lack understanding of what happened and how God will deal with us. So, once we get enough nerve to answer when He calls for our attention, we begin to point fingers. We blame everyone in an attempt to save ourselves, failing to recognize that God knows the whole truth. He seeks to see how honest we will be with Him and ourselves.

God did with Adam and Eve what He does with us. He made an animal sacrifice that day to cover their sins and their bodies and brought them back into the right relationship with Him. He sent Christ to die for us, to save us from sin and get us back into the right relationship with Him. They suffered consequences for their actions. Yet, He showed them grace, mercy, and love because they did not die immediately. The enemy also received his punishment that day; part of it is that God put enmity between him and the woman (verse 15). Which means there is mutual hate between the enemy and the woman.

Stand Against the Opponent

In the face of opposition from the devil, we as believers must stand firm and resolute, armed with knowledge and spiritual discernment. Recognizing the means of operation employed by the devil is the first step toward safeguarding our souls. By understanding the devil's tactics, we can develop a heightened awareness of the temptations and deceptions that may come our way. This awareness enables us to be vigilant and discerning, actively resisting the enticements that lead us astray from our values and beliefs. It empowers us to make conscious choices and decisions that align with our higher purpose and spiritual well-being.

Ephesians 6:10-11 says, "Finally, my brethren, be strong in the Lord, and in the power of his might. Put on the whole armor of God, that ye may be able **to stand against the wiles of the devil**" (boldness added for emphasis). We must recognize that the devil is a roaring lion seeking whom he may devour- 1 Peter 5:8. When we place on God's whole armor, we can stand against all the ploys, plots, tricks, traps, and temptations the devil throws in our path. If he can distract us, he can gain access and devour us. We must always be suited up. By doing so, we block his entry. Meaning even if he seeks to devour us, he can't. He can only consume those that are accessible.

Standing against the opponent requires a strong foundation, faith, and inner strength. By nurturing a deep connection with God, we can tap into a source of guidance and protection. This connection allows us to draw upon the wisdom and strength necessary to resist the devil's advances. It empowers us to rely on prayer, meditation, reading, and studying God's Word and other spiritual practices that fortify our souls and keep us rooted in the light. Through steadfast faith and a commitment to righteousness, we can stand firm against the opposition posed by the devil, safeguarding our souls and maintaining a steady connection with our Heavenly Father.

Friends, please remember that people are not our enemies, but the actual enemy will use people to oppose us, steal from us, destroy us, or even kill us. When we give him access, we give him the power to use us as tools to do his evil work. Ephesians 6:12 (KJV) tells us, "We wrestle not against flesh and blood, but against principalities, against powers, against the rulers of the darkness of this world, against spiritual wickedness in high places." Again, people are not our enemies. We have a real spiritual enemy who loves it when we battle and accuse and choose not to forgive each other. We must recognize when the enemy uses others as his tools to do his bidding. Satan is not omnipresent. He cannot be everywhere like God. He needs help. We must not allow him to use us but be aware that he does use people to do his work. We must not let anything or anyone in our lives have the power to cause us to act out of character, rob us of our peace, or destroy our integrity. Satan can use believers as tools when we fail to be in alignment with God. That is why we must pay attention to his means of operation and be intentional about putting on the whole armor of God each day and every day, all day.

The Enemy's Means of Operation

Come – he comes to us while we are vulnerable.

Pose – pretend to be what is not.

Suggest – put a particular thought in our mind.

Deceive – mislead us even with the truth.

Entice – tempt.

Expose – take away or lead us away from the protection of God.

Leave – depart from us, set us up to die.

Satan uses the same M.O. (means of operation) with us today as in the Garden of Eden with Adam and Eve. Now that we know how he operates, we should be able to block many of his punches. Even

the ones that do connect, we should not be faded by them. They will lack the power to cause harm or damage, even injury. It may sting, but it will not dislocate anything. We can still stand and throw our own combinations of jabs and crosses.

STRENGTHS AND WEAKNESS

Understanding satan's strengths and weaknesses is crucial when mastering spiritual warfare. They let us know his tactics and strategies, enabling us to stand firm and resist his attacks. By studying his patterns, we gain insight into his deceptive nature and become better equipped to discern his lies, temptations, and schemes. This awareness empowers us to rely on the power of God, employ spiritual weapons, and walk in the authority granted to us as believers, ultimately leading to victory in spiritual battles.

Strengths

The enemy is very clever. He is resourceful. He is witty and marked by ingenuity. He is no dummy. The enemy is slick and quick. He does not stand around being idle. He is always on the move. He has a unique ability to lead and get people to follow him. He is a charlatan – imposter, so you never know in what shape, form, person, place, possession, passion, or pleasure he may appear as. We must be alert at all times. He is persistent.

Weakness

What is his weakness? The Word of God. The name of Jesus. Period! We are no match for the devil alone. We need Jesus and God's Word. Don't believe me? Let us look quickly at how the Word defeats him.

When the tempter came to Him, he said, "If You are the Son of God, command that these stones become bread." But He answered and said, "It is written, 'Man shall not live by bread alone, but every word that proceeds from the mouth of God.'"- (Matthew 4: 3-4).

ACCESS DENIED

I have a saying that reminds me not to give the enemy a foothold in my life. I often say, access denied, security clearance revoked. We have zero business together. As Jesus told Peter in Matthew 16:22-23, this is my way of saying, "Get behind Me, satan!" I repeat this phrase out loud each time I recognize the workings of the enemy in certain situations. When I became intentional about bringing my thoughts under captivity for the obedience of Christ (see 2 Corinthians 10:5), a shift took place. I understood that once satan enters your mind, he controls your actions. I was determined not to allow that to happen to me again.

As a follower of Christ, I have encountered many believers who speak about satan as if they are familiar with him. Yet, much like myself, they continue to fall short of God's glory because they sink deep into traps the enemy sets before them. This was me at one time (both hands raised). I, too, have fallen for the okie-doke many times. I can say boldly after my last fall, I vowed to learn all I needed to know about my enemy to come out victorious when I go head-to-head with him. I promised to decline any and everything and everyone that is connected to him. My motto is, "Access denied, security clearance revoked, we have zero business together." I am committed to denying the enemy access to my life. By the end of this book, I pray you will make the same commitment.

My friends, we can no longer allow the enemy to control any part of our thoughts. We must deny satan access to our thoughts, which is crucial for overcoming adversity and healing from emotional wounds. By guarding our minds and refusing to entertain negative and destructive thoughts, we create a safe space for positive thinking, resilience, and growth. It allows us to break free from the chains of negativity, embrace hope, and experience the transformative power of God's love and healing in our lives.

Satan seeks to kill, steal, and destroy believers by manipulating their thoughts and taking advantage of adverse situations and circumstances. He plants seeds of doubt, fear, and despair through his schemes, seeking to rob us of our joy, peace, and faith. He capitalizes on vulnerable moments to distort the truth, sow discord, and hinder spiritual growth, aiming to undermine our relationship with God and our ability to fulfill our purpose. The key to denying him access and overcoming him is to take our thoughts captive. Friends, I urge you to recognize the devil's tactics, arm yourselves with God's armor, stand firm in your faith, and actively combat satan's attacks with the truth of God's Word, prayer, and reliance on the Holy Spirit. It is time to level up!

CHAPTER TWO

THE STRATEGY

During this GAP season, I recognized the connection between spiritual and personal growth and its impact on cultivating and maintaining mental and emotional health. Taking notice of the connection between the two was instrumental in healing past emotional wounds. Spiritual growth provides a framework for understanding and transcending our pain and suffering, while personal growth empowers us to confront and address our emotional wounds directly. By exploring our spirituality, we tap into a source of wisdom, guidance, and unconditional love that can support our healing journey. Spiritual practices such as prayer, meditation, Bible reading, Scripture memorization, praise, and worship aided me. It will help you connect with a deeper level of self-awareness and provide solace as you navigate to the depths of your emotional wounds.

On the other hand, personal growth invites us to examine our past experiences, beliefs, and patterns that contribute to our emotional wounds. It encourages self-reflection, self-compassion, and the willingness to face our pain head-on. Through personal growth, we develop the tools and resources to heal our emotional wounds. This may involve seeking therapy, engaging in self-help practices, or seeking support from a trusted community. By actively working on our personal growth, we gain the insight and resilience necessary to process and release past emotional wounds, fostering a greater sense of mental and emotional well-being and wholeness.

The connections between spiritual and personal growth and healing past emotional injuries lie in the shared emphasis on forgiveness, acceptance, and inner transformation. Spirituality invites us to cultivate forgiveness- for ourselves and others – allowing us to release the burdens of resentment and anger that often accompany emotional injuries. Personal growth, in turn, encourages us to accept our healing and inner peace.

I began my healing journey by integrating spiritual and personal growth practices during this GAP season. I developed the RAY (Realign and Yield) Process as a comprehensive approach to addressing my emotional wounds. The spiritual practices I implemented provided a sense of wholeness, meaning, and connectedness. At the same time, personal growth empowered me to take responsibility for my healing and actively engage in the necessary inner work. Together, they formed a powerful combination that supported my healing process, allowing me to reclaim my emotional well-being and move forward with a renewed sense of purpose and wholeness during one of the most challenging seasons of my life.

STRATEGY

I shared in the introduction that this book is my testimony to my broken surrender and coming into complete agreement with God. A statement of how I gained freedom and power in a challenging and trying circumstance. Now I want to share my process for allowing God to filter out my impurities and fill me with His Truth. In the process, I had to face off with myself. I had to resolve to get out of my own way. In the process, I had to give up my way of thinking about past events and my current situation that had an adverse impact on my life. I gave up my way of viewing myself for how God views me. I chose to take on God's Truth to replace negative thought patterns that distorted my view of life and cultivated the l.o.v.e. (liberty over vulnerable emotions) mindset.

The RAY Process is my fight plan – a soul care treatment plan. An action plan that helped me upgrade on power during the fight. I had to take my thoughts captive and surrender my old way of viewing trouble, trials, and tribulations. Freedom and strength came as I let go of the impurities – past pain, fear, guilt, shame, doubt, and unforgiveness, and allowed God to refine poor character traits. I had to relinquish the things that kept me from proper progression and living in the here and now. Living in the abundance Christ promised in John 10:10. Surrendering required the reconstruction of core beliefs, thinking patterns, and speech to align with God's values. By giving up the old for the new, I recognized and accepted that "Who the Son makes free is truly free indeed" (John 8:36). The RAY Process allowed me to receive freedom and what I need to shine in the darkness, to power up and to rise to the next level. It jump-started my journey to personal holiness and the cultivation of the l.o.v.e mindset, which included true healing as I feel-deal-heal and got up off the canvas after being knocked down.

*Ray: a thin beam of radiant energy (as light).

Once, your life was full of sin's darkness, but now you have the very light of our LORD shining through you because of your union with Him. Your mission is to live as a child flooded with His revelation – light (Ephesians 5:8).

THE RAY PROCESS

1. **Recognize**: Conduct a self-assessment to identify the areas in your life that are not in alignment with the things of God. Acknowledge that you need to prioritize things you need to change, areas for growth, and what must be let go. This may include wrong/negative thoughts, improper/damaging relationships, behaviors, negative attitudes, and blatant character flaws. Things that satan uses as strongholds.

2. **Reconcile**: Accept the truth of what you identified during your assessment. Determine to have a willing mind that you will embrace help. Prepare yourself for learning new things. Prepare yourself for change.

3. **Rededicate**: Decide to live a life set apart for God's purpose. Invite Christ to come back into your life as LORD and Savior. Reposition (align, prioritize) your values, thoughts, beliefs, actions, and way of doing things so that God is number one.

4. **Relinquish**: Let go of all profane -sinful things (people, places, possessions, pleasures, and passions). Anything that contributes to living outside of God's will. Give up the old so you can make room for the new. For example, let go of the old lies about yourself and replace them with new truths – God's Truth.

5. **Reclaim**: Learn and apply new biblical principles and positive and adaptive coping methods. Make the decision to live according to what God says. Embrace the new because you have already given up the old. Choose to live godly, set apart (sanctified in thoughts, speech, and actions). Own your identity as a child of the True and Living God. Profess that Jesus is LORD and make all necessary changes to demonstrate such a claim in every aspect of your life. I call it radical obedience.

6. **Refine**: Work to improve and enhance your Spiritual maturity. Study, read, and meditate on God's Word daily. Sharpen your Spiritual weapons of warfare (scripture, song praise, meditation, memorization, worship). These things strengthen faith. They also enhance character and change in thought, speech, and actions. How you view and handle problems manifested from adequately using these weapons and your spiritual maturity. The desire to do things the King's way instead of your way is displayed.

7. **Release**: Allow the power of love and faith to flow and free you. By making the proper alignment, the spirit and soul are now connected,

and the Spirit can release God's DNA into the soul bringing about total transformation into the person God designed you to be. Bring about the ability to endure with complete faith that God is in control of your life and any problems you face. Release the power of faith into your situations and circumstances and watch God do amazing things in it, in you, and through you.

Soul care is a tactical strategy to aid healing and maintenance after recovery. Soul care assists in preventing strongholds by eliminating toxic waste buildup and overcoming them before emotional injuries lead to gapping, infected holes in your soul. Soul care is a method to address character defects, rid our souls of toxic waste, and renew our minds. You must be willing to address emotional disruptions, emotional damage, and spiritual damage that contributes to toxic thoughts, speech, and behavior. Be ready to handle the things that have you bound and keep you from being the person God has designed you to be. Address the issues of life with the confidence of God.

Friends' soul care helps us to remain connected to the Spirit and maintain the l.o.v.e mindset. For our spirit and soul to agree, the soul must be healed. Many times, that beings with cleaning up our thought life. Allowing God's Word to purge toxic statements and lies fills us with the truth. I would like to walk you through each phase so you may have a more practical understanding of how to apply this process in your life – that is, if you choose to do so. In doing so, you will not only level up over the enemy, and you will shine as you go.

LEVEL UP PLAYLIST

All that knows me knows I enjoy dancing and listening to music. Music is a powerful tool for aiding the healing process. It is a source of inspiration, encouragement and fosters a connection with something greater than oneself. Unfortunately, during my incarceration, this helpful tool was stripped from us. During the COVID pandemic at the beginning of 2021, the administration decided to remove batteries from the commissary, therefore, deeming radios obsolete and failing to

acknowledge the adverse effect the decision would have on the mental state of a fragile sub-population.

In the context of a holding facility – a jail, where detainees are already experiencing a challenging and uncertain environment, removing music without regard to its impact can be deeply detrimental. Music has the power to provide emotional release, offer a temporary escape from distressing circumstances, and foster a sense of hope and resilience. Depriving detainees of access to music not only robs them of a valuable coping mechanism but also disregards their emotional well-being and strips away a source of comfort and humanity in an already difficult situation.

Each morning I would wake up with a song in my head. I deemed it my song of the day. Whenever I felt a negative mood shift or needed words of encouragement, I would begin to sing the song to refocus my attention on the things of God. My song of the day would help me enter God's presence and remember His promises.

This playlist is a mixture of songs I would sing in some variation daily to aid me. I could not remember the entire song, but it did not stop me from singing anyway. Sometimes, I would ask my husband to play music during our calls, or I would have him print lyrics and send them to me. The lyrics gave me solace and hope and encouraged me to keep fighting. Some helped me to enter into God's presence and worship Him. These songs have helped me as I journey through healing and renewal. The words in each song kept me pressing forward and claiming victory. These are my fight songs. Now that I am home, I use this tool to aid me in the recovery process as I continue to remain kingdom focused and fight until the final bell sounds. Are you ready? Turn up the volume, and let's fight.

Deliver Me - Donald Lawrence
and Le'Andria Johnson

I Got That – Anthony Brown
& group therAPy

No Weapon – Fred Hammond

Can't Give Up Now -Mary Mary

Break Every Chain – Tasha Cobbs Leonard

I'm Getting Read – Tasha Cobbs Leonard

Never Would Have Made It – Marvin Sapp

I Need You Now – Smokie Norful

I Trust You – James Fortune & Fiya

This Week – Anthony Brown & group therAPy

Worth – Anthony Brown & group therAPy

Gorilla Faith – Deitrick Haddon

I Won't Go Back – William McDowell

He Has His Hands On You –
Marvin Sapp

The Battle Is The Lord's –
Yolanda Adams

BIG – Pastor Mike Jr.

Give Me You – Shana Wilson-Williams

Greater Is Coming – Jekalyn Carr

My Testimony – Marvin Sapp

The Best In Me – Marvin Sapp

Bigger – Jekalyn Carr

Unstoppable – Koryn Hawthorne

Intentional – Travis Greene

Change Me – Tamela Mann

Thank You For It All – Marvin Sapp

It's Working – William Murphy

For My Good – Todd Galberth

It Ain't Over – Maurette Brown Clark

Encourage Yourself- Sheri Jones - Moffett

Holy Water – Tasha Cobbs Leonard
and We the Kingdom

SCRIPTURES OF STRENGTH

Embracing scriptures that speak about strength can be a powerful source of inspiration during challenging times. These sacred verses offer guidance and encouragement, reminding us of our inner resilience and capacity to overcome adversity. By immersing ourselves in the wisdom and teachings of the scriptures, we can find solace, courage, and the motivation needed to face difficult situations head-on. In times of struggle, turning to these holy words can provide a sense of hope and help us navigate the storms of life with renewed strength and remain Kingdom-focused in the process. The following is a list of Scriptures that aid in restoring my strength and focus.

Philippians 4:13	Isaiah 40:31
Isaiah 41:10	Isaiah 40:29-31
Ephesians 6:10	Isaiah 43:2
Psalms 119:28	Psalms 46:1
2 Timothy 1:7	Psalms 59:16
Psalms 18:1-2	Psalms 118:14
John 16:33	Psalms 27:1
Psalms 29:11	Psalms 73:26
2 Corinthians 12:9-10	1 Corinthians 16:13
Psalms 22:19	Psalms 28:7-8
Nehemiah 8:10	Habakkuk 3:19
Exodus 15:2	1 Chronicles 16:11
Deuteronomy 20:4	Deuteronomy 31:6
Jeremiah 32:17	Joshua 1:9

CHAPTER THREE

RECOGNIZE

Throughout my professional career and during my GAP season, I have learned the necessity of conducting a self-assessment. This should be done with unflinching honesty. It is vital to turn our gaze inward, peering into the depths of our being, seeking to understand our strengths and weaknesses and the intricate nuances that shape our existence. Root issues must be dealt with for healing to take place. Many do not receive healing because the process requires facing off with self. It means becoming vulnerable and being open and honest about the "scary" things. Those things we suppressed and buried, hoping they would never surface. Sadly, we fail to realize or recognize that they do resurface. In ways that show up in our attitudes, thought patterns, speech, and behaviors. The fruit we bear is tainted, toxic, unusable, and unholy.

Unresolved pain turns into heart matters. As believers, we know that God judges our hearts 1 Samuel 16:7; Proverbs 16:2). We will address issues of the heart shortly. My point is that deep seeded toxins infect our entire being. We must move away from not wanting to address or avoiding those things that make us uncomfortable or scare us. Avoiding what scares you means that what scares you is what is in control of you. You can replace scared with words such as anger, disappoints, hurts/pains, etc.

I have come to understand that the root of most people's unresolved healing is pain, fear, or both. For example, a person who has difficulty managing the intense emotion of anger. The root of that anger is either pain, fear, or both. Anger is secondary to the primary. Until the primary issues are identified and addressed, the roots will remain, which causes the weeds to grow and take over the wheat (positive). Are you ready to separate the wheat (positive thoughts) from the weeds (negative thoughts)? This process is not easy, but necessary to not be knocked out by the opponent (the devil). Weeds (negative thoughts) contribute to you having a blindside. They impact your energy level, impairing your ability to keep your hands up so you can defend yourself.

My friends, we must acknowledge and admit our areas of weakness and flaws. To deny that we do not have it all together is exactly what satan wants us to do. To live in a false reality, denying the truth, when we pretend to have it all together, we lie to ourselves and others. This causes a rift, and we lack the ability to be open and honest in our relationships. It causes a disconnect in our relationship with Christ and deprives us of our truth regarding who we are, why we are here, and how to overcome things that keep us from holy living and a life of abundance. It is our responsibility to recognize the shortcomings and correct them to deny satan access to our lives. Some things we cannot do alone. It requires God, and He may assign others to aid us.

We must acknowledge that the pain is too difficult to handle alone. Pain from what? Past trauma, problems, situations, and circumstances that we still carry. Pain from current trials and tribulations we endure. Fear attached to situations. Stress from the consequences of our choices. Troubles that come from giving in to temptation. We must recognize the need to let go and rise above the past. We must recognize and acknowledge the need for help to overcome the trials and temptations of the present. Recognize our current stance and view of life. If it does not align with God's way of living, we must acknowledge the need to change.

I recognize that for some of us, our struggles and suffering sometimes become the most familiar components of our lives. We normalize them to the point that we have a hard time imagining life without struggle or suffering. Pain becomes a part of our routine and explanation for inadequacies. It consumes our time and attention, even our identity. The bottom line, we must recognize our need for God in our lives – in every aspect. We must accept that we cannot do life without Him. We cannot overcome and next level without Him. Jesus came to next level of us, and we must accept His assistance. Knowing that there are so many benefits to joining Team Jesus.

In the recognition phase, we should begin to spend more time with Jesus. This was when I asked my friend Lashond to send me a Bible. When I received it, I started reading from the beginning. I read the entire Bible, word for word, in two months. Every chance I got to read, that is what I was doing. As I read, I began to gain insight, and honestly, life (energy) began to increase. The more I read, the more I wanted and needed to know.

As my reading increased, so did my prayer life. I began to take notes and ask questions. The light bulb came on, and its brightness increased. I was able to see again. God revealed Himself to me in a new way on a new level. I was excited and renewed by what He was showing me. However, some things He presented, I was not ready to accept. God showed me the fragmented me. I had to deal with the things I was being shown to move to the next level. I trusted Him, and I received the truth being shown to me. I accepted that this trial was allowed, but the reason was not revealed. I recognized and acknowledged my lack of understanding. I also realized that posing the "Why?" question only leads to a cycle of frustration. That was the last thing I needed. So, I decided to explore how to survive this season as my inner desire to thrive burned.

Trials may come because of consequences related to our choices. That was my struggle. I had sinned against God. As a result, poor decisions led to my incarceration. Being forced to deal with hardships caused by your own actions or not is a hard pill to swallow. My pain and lack of understanding drove me to search for knowledge to relieve the pain. The question of how I handle this and remain sane was posed. As I conducted a self-assessment, I recognized four key areas I had to address to survive this GAP season – trials, temptations, wrong thinking, and core beliefs.

RECOGNIZING TRIALS

Please understand that in this life, we will experience hardships, problems, and unpleasant and uncomfortable situations that cause pain (physical, mental) and emotional distress. We must recognize how those things impact our way of functioning. If our life does not align with what God says, we must stop at that moment and decide to address the issue before it gets out of hand. Just because we encounter life's woes does not mean they have to control us.

I have suffered through the death of my oldest son (November 8, 2019), approximately seven months after being incarcerated for the first time. Mourning the death of my first-born son while incarcerated, without being able to say goodbye, is an incredible and heart-wrenching experience that I wish on no one. It is a profound loss that pierces the soul, leaving a void that cannot be filled. The weight of grief is magnified by the inability to be present in the moment of farewell, to be offered comfort or offer comfort, and to share the pain with loved ones. In this painful journey of mourning the death of my oldest son, there was a sense of guilt, regret, and longing for what could have been.

During such deep grief and sorrow, it was vital for me to find solace in the arms of my loving heavenly Father and the support of others. Physical support was limited, but I was able to share some of the pain with two others who experienced similar losses. Thank you, Faith and Grace. You know who you are. I also sought solace in prayer and meditation and received comfort from the Holy Spirit.

The loss of my home and other material possessions (2020), and the death of my daddy (2021), all while grieving the end of my life as I knew it was not an easy feat but manageable because I learned how to lean on God after my son's death. I learned good grief and how to move forward by faith. I also endured illness, not even recognizing that I was in critical condition because the medical staff at the jail and hospital did not deem me worthy enough to give me details about my health condition. I have even suffered mistreatment by staff, but through it all, God helped me to tap into the peace Jesus gave me. I have joy amid the storm. I have peace that surpasses all understanding because I recognized and acknowledged the need to change my perspective, which changed my thoughts about what I suffered.

I also learned that trials test my faith, build me up, and enhance my character if allowed. You and I can have joy during hardship because we know we are being changed into a stronger and wiser version of ourselves.

Be assured that the testing of your faith [through experience] produces endurance [leading to spiritual maturity and inner peace] James 1:3 (AMP).

Trials may come because of consequences related to our choices. They may come because of no fault or ours. An example is COVID (sickness) not caused by our way of living. COVID has caused distress in so many areas of life. The devil uses such situations to strike fear into those who give him access. This burdens the individual even more because of unnecessary worry-related stress. So how should we handle the various trials of life? James tells us to:

Consider it nothing but joy…whenever you fall into various trials – James 1:2 (AMP).

Yes, you read it correctly. No, I did not misquote what Paul said. So, what does he mean by "consider it nothing but joy?" The first word of the verse tells us to give careful attention to the issue at hand. Think about it from the perspective of joy. It is about how we think and view the situation that impacts us most.

We must get our minds right to have joy even during suffering. As children of God, we can have joy and peace even in the most challenging and complex situations. Our perspective and thoughts make the difference between us having or not having. I have them both during this storm as I write this book. I am in the thick of things, but my joy and peace remain. I am in a season filled with grief and pain, lack and loss, yet I still have peace and joy. How? I yielded – recognition. I recognized and acknowledged the truth and the Truth.

Yes, during the fight (spiritual warfare), we must recognize that we are being tested. Each trial, tribulation, storm, struggle, etc., is a test. Our faith is being tested. What we say, what we believe are examined when we endure suffering. Our belief in God and the teachings of Jesus is being challenged and evaluated in our lives. Do we really trust Him, or are we speaking words that sound good and doing things to make us look like we believe, but it is all empty, "a show?"

Secondly, our character is being refined. Each test brings about self-improvement so that we can think, look, act, and be more like Christ. How we respond under the force and pressure of trials provides us with knowledge of our sincerity regarding our spiritual knowing and maturity. If we pay attention to how we respond to suffering, hardship, and life woes, we will know our true level of faith. Proper knowledge and application of that knowledge lead us to grow in our trust in God. It gives us peace that only God can provide us with. This peace is given during the fight. It also leads to original character building, which offers more power. We become more and more like Jesus, which provides even more power.

My friends, when we change our perspective regarding the trials of life, we increase in power when that focus is on Jesus. The joy that comes from the Lord is strength – Nehemiah 8:10. Level up over trials with joy and peace.

RECOGNIZING TEMPTATION

Recognizing temptation during healing is vital to our journey toward wholeness and spiritual growth. As we navigate the path of healing, we may encounter moments of vulnerability and weakness where the allure of familiar but unhealthy patterns beckons. We must be vigilant and discerning in these moments, acknowledging the temptations that arise. We must also identify and recognize past temptations that led us astray and contributed to past and current pain and distress. By recognizing these temptations, we can actively resist them and instead embrace the path of healing, growth, and righteousness.

It is important to remember that God does not impart evil upon us but instead allows it for two reasons: for the progression of the gospel or due to our free will – volition. Some things we suffer are because of the natural order of things in this world once sin entered and disrupted God's order. Secondly, God's divine love for us grants us the freedom to make choices, even though some may lead us astray.

Our journey of healing involves navigating the consequences of our actions and the presence of evil in the environments and world around us. Through God's grace and the guidance of the Holy Spirit, we can find the strength to resist temptation and walk in alignment with God's will. God's loving presence in our lives enables us to overcome the allure of temptation, transforming our weaknesses into opportunities for growth and drawing us close to the light of His Truth and healing.

Side note: There is a misguided saying I would like to address., "God will not put no more on you than you can bear." Says who? That is not biblical truth. Ask Paul and those who traveled with him. He will tell you that he suffered many things that were too much to bear, and God allowed him to suffer those things for the gospel's progression.

My friends, I want you to know what a hard time we had in Asia. Our sufferings were so horrible and so unbearable that death seemed certain – 2 Corinthians 1:8 (CEV)

There we have it. We can suffer to the point where it is too much to handle. Think about it, Paul felt that way, and he was doing the work of the Lord. For us who suffer because of our choices that do not align with God's Word, you must know that stuffing can get heavy and rough. Like Paul and his crew, we must extend our hands and request help from the Lord, or despair will become so heavy we will wish for death to relieve us from its grip. Therefore, God will not allow too much to be upon us that He can't handle. God also gives a way of escape according to 1 Corinthians 10:12-13. Sadly, many of us do not use the escape route.

God will not allow us to be tempted too much. The temptation will come. God will determine how much is too much and give us a way out. The invitation to temptation may be extended, but God gives us a reason not to RSVP – accept the invite. As believers, we must recognize that we are not exempt from being tempted. Come on now; even Jesus was tempted, so we never thought we would not be.

We must understand that we are tempted by the ordinary things of man – people, places, possessions, passions, and pleasures. The things that satisfy the sensual – carnal part of our fleshy being. However, God being faithful provides us with a way out to maintain our spiritual nature. In giving the exit, He does not deny us our free will. We have a choice to partake or to pass. James put it this way in chapter one, verses 14-15:

We are tempted by our own desires that drag us off and trap us. Our desires make us sin, and when sin is finished with us, it leaves us dead- (CEV).

FYI, God does NOT tempt us. God cannot tempt us because He cannot be tempted by evil, and He Himself tempts no one – James 1:13. Don't blame God when you are tempted. It is not God's fault. We have already identified the tempter in chapter one. He tempts us according to our desires. If our desires are Godly, then he – the tempter – has nothing to draw us with. He does not have the power.

However, if we crave the things of the world, he uses those desires to get us to seek out and fulfill the lustful impulses to gain access to our lives. His goal is to steal, to kill, and to destroy. My friends, to level up over our opponent, we must identify our desires and deficiencies.

First, we must identify our desires and see if they align with God's desires for our lives. We are the weakest link when our desires lean towards worldly profane things and pleasure and engage in satisfying ourselves. We are the weakest link when our inner self is unstable. Profane living keeps us on the enemy's level. Sanctified living causes us to level up. Our desires must be purified if they are not of God. He will give us our heart's desires if we live according to His Word.

> *Delight yourselves also in the Lord, and He shall give you the desires of your heart. – Psalm 37:4 (NKJV).*

No more wanting what the world wants. I am not saying God does not want us to have money, cars, and clothes. These should not be our sole purpose or focus in life. They should not be so important that if we do not have them, our world is turned upside down, and we lose our minds. That goes for anything that we place before God.

Secondly, we must identify our deficiencies. Friends, we are triune beings; we will discuss this in detail later. For now, I would like to share that we are made of spirit, soul, and body. Our body houses our soul and spirit. It also gives us a sensual connection to the world. When our flesh strongly influences our soul, it provides satan easy access to our lives. Therefore, when we have a deficit in any area of our life - spiritual, physical, recreational, intellectual, financial, or emotional - the devil will send something or someone to fulfill that area. He aims to use that something or someone to aid us in self-assassination. We fail to recognize the red flags or discern God's voice, making decisions that lead to self-destruction. Friends, we have to be aware of the empty spaces in our lives. We must acknowledge the areas of deficiency and allow God to fill them so we may resist temptation easily.

Friends, we must recognize our desires and deficiencies and release them to God to level up over temptations.

RECOGNIZING WRONG MINDSETS

We develop wrong mindsets when we allow trials and temptations to consume us. Recognizing harmful or inaccurate perspectives is a crucial step toward emotional healing. It involves developing self-awareness and acknowledging the destructive patterns of thinking and belief systems that contribute to emotional distress. By shining light on these negative mindsets, we can challenge them and explore healthier alternatives. Change is necessary because negative attitudes perpetuate self-sabotage, self-doubt, and emotional pain, creating barriers to healing and growth. There are several negative or wrong mindsets that, when addressed and changed, will pave the way for emotional healing to occur. Some of these include:

Double-minded: wavering between faith and fear; knowing what is right and doing it; pleasing self while trying to please God.

Judgmental minded: judging wrongly; offshoot or negative mind — thinking about what is wrong with an individual to include self.

Negative minded: see only the bad; denial or refusal for truth; all or nothing thinking pattern.

Perfectionism: holding oneself to impossibly high standards and constantly striving for perfection. Generating feelings of inadequacy and self-criticism.

Prejudice minded: having an unreasonable attitude.

Self-limiting beliefs: negative beliefs about oneself.

Victim mentality: believing one is powerless and constantly subjected to adverse circumstances.

This is not an all-inclusive list. It is just an example of how far we can stray from the right path when we give the devil access to our thoughts. These mindsets cause us to think wrongly about God, others, and ourselves. Trials will come, but we must remain alert enough not to allow satan to take advantage of us in our moments of weakness. During hard times, we must acquire and maintain the right mindset, Jesus mindset, Word mindset, and love mindset. By doing so, we deliver a powerful right hook to satan. KO! By addressing and transforming these negative or wrong mindsets, we create a more nurturing and empowering internal environment, paving the way for emotional healing and personal growth, which gives us what it takes to level up.

RECOGNIZING CORE BELIEFS

Core beliefs are convictions that form the foundation for how we view the world and guide our understanding of reality, meaning, and purpose. These beliefs are our thoughts, values, attitudes, and behaviors. They are deeply ingrained. Core beliefs serve as a compass that navigates how we interpret challenges and woes in life. They provide a sense of identity, stability, and coherence, shaping how we perceive ourselves, others, and the world. Core beliefs, ultimately, reflect our deeply held convictions and shape our actions and the choices we make according to how we see the world.

I had to identify and accept the convictions I had developed out of bad experiences that connected to why I was moving differently. Why was I making choices that did not align with my true identity and values? I made a connection that helped me to understand how my beliefs and thoughts influenced my speech, actions, and character. This was vital to setting me on the path to healing. Allowing me to identify patterns and dynamics shaping my behavior and interactions with others and leading me to greater authenticity. Friends, it is paramount that you recognize flawed core beliefs that impede your progress toward healing and contribute to self-destructive patterns of behavior.

Recognizing the impact of thought patterns, core beliefs, and temptations is vital to change our perception in the face of life's trials.

Our thoughts and opinions shape our perspectives and influence how we interpret and respond to challenging situations. By becoming aware of negative or limiting thought patterns, we can actively challenge and replace them with positive and empowering thoughts. Similarly, identifying and addressing core beliefs rooted in fear, doubt, or self-limitation allows us to transform our mindset and embrace a more resilient and optimistic outlook. Additionally, recognizing and resisting temptations that seek to draw us away from the truth and alignment with our values enables us to maintain clarity, integrity, and spiritual strength amid trials. These practices empower us to shift our perception, cultivate resilience, and find growth and purpose even in the most challenging circumstances.

Scriptures of Strength

Philippians 4:13 Isaiah 40:31

Isaiah 41:10 Isaiah 40:29-31

CHAPTER FOUR

RECONCILE

We must get to know ourselves before we move forward and cause the enemy to bite the dust (no pun intended). We must identify the foundation of our identity and understand how it impacts our spiritual and personal growth. We must understand why the enemy is adamant about focusing on us. Why is he all up in our business? Trust me, it is not because he thinks you and I are cute or wants to be our friend.

I know from personal and professional experience that some situations in life are so painful they leave many emotional wounds and scars that impact our current view of ourselves. These experiences have shaped how we show up in life based on our self-perspective. Many people are walking around with false perceptions – persona and façade – of their identities. Every day they believe the hype and lies the enemy has told them. Many are in bad relationships because they do not know who they are. Some have been mentally, emotionally, and physically incarcerated due to too many compromises.

WAKING SELF-DISCOVERY

Who Am I?

Much like we sought out information to know all we could about the opposition, we must learn all we can about ourselves. Trust, the devil has done his homework. Knowing and accepting the truth about our authentic identity allows us to develop a sense of self-awareness.

We clearly understand our strengths, weaknesses, values, beliefs, aspirations, expectations, and perceptions. This self-awareness enables us to live authentically, aligning our thoughts, actions, choices, and relationships with our true selves. We cultivate genuine confidence and inner harmony by embracing our authentic identity. Something we all need.

Embracing our authentic identity will also aid us with navigating the trials and tribulations we face in life and no longer allow satan to use them to his advantage. So, let's get started by asking ourselves a fundamental question: Who am I?

Recognizing the need for my clients to understand and identify their identity as it relates to maintaining mental and emotional stability, I intentionally assigned a therapeutic assignment titled "Who Am I." Each client had the task of describing themself. I posed the same question to myself over the years as well. I was so confident in my response. I listed all my roles, qualities, skills, etc. I even had at the top of the list, "I am a child of God." However, I needed to recognize the depth of that statement. I lacked accurate knowledge of who I was because I lacked a proper understanding of the power in the statement, "I am a child of God." I lacked significant insight into who I was according to what God said. Oh, but now! Come on, Jesus!

Friends, I was she who was in the wrong relationships because I based my identity on the wrong things. Therefore, when those things no longer existed, I became lost, confused, and doubtful of my worth. Through my healing process, I learned a lot about myself. Because I am healed, I can share this with you without feeling guilt, shame, or fear. I sought validation from the men I was in a relationship with. I was broken and did not know who I was. The lack of knowledge caused me to compromise my values, worth, and standards, and I settled just to be settling. I became stagnant, stuck, and even more emotionally damaged. My lack of identity contributed to my living outside of God's will. It also caused me to function below the level God planned for me to operate on, and I was not she who He called and created me to be.

From the beginning, the enemy planned to keep us from knowing our true identity. He specializes in casting doubt and attacking our minds through manipulative thoughts, ideas, and suggestions. Remember Eve? He tricked her out of paradise with shrewd suggestions. Friends, we must stay alert and be ready to bob and weave. We must not be ignorant of his devices according to 2 Corinthians 2:11 – Lest satan should take advantage of us; for we are not ignorant of his devices (NKJV).

Ask yourself, "Who am I?" Take a few moments to jot down what comes to your mind. Please think about the question in depth. It is important. You can only level up and stay there if you do. Satan knows our proclivities, hangups, mistakes, and things we are hiding in the dark, secrets. Remember, the deceiver operates in darkness. He wants us to remain ignorant of our true identity.

Did you answer the question? I will give you a hint – you are a child of God. Having a complete understanding of what it means to be a child of God and operate (live) by that knowledge makes you and I a threat to the enemy. So, he does all that he can to keep us from genuinely obtaining the facts and accepting our position in God's family. He wants to rob you of that knowledge so that you will not grow and live in the fullness of all the rights and privileges of a member of the Royal Family. To do so means you have the power to bring down satan's kingdom. To destroy what he has built. To take back the things that he stole from us—God's children, at the beginning in the Garden of Eden all the way up until this very moment of you holding and reading this book.

My friends satan is livid because you are reading this book. Much like he was as I was writing it. Trust me, it came with challenges, distractions, and more. However, because I now know who I am, whose I am, and the enemy's M.O., I was able to power through with the power within me. We will talk more about that power later. Let's finish discovering who you are. Let's tackle some critical areas to deal with so that you can become the person God created you to be. We must address root issues—emotional wounds that have caused you to have a blindside (damage) that the devil can, will, or is using to take advantage of you and keep you on the ropes so you cannot fight back. Please note, to come out of the corner and get back to the center of the ring, you will have to move on from the pain caused by people, places, possessions, pleasures, and passions that contributed to the emotional injuries that still have you bound to the past. A lack of healing is a significant blind spot. Recovery must take place for you to level up as I did and continue to do so. It is the proper way to be aware and be whole. In my most famous words, "You must feel, deal, and heal." Well, when it comes to the subject of mental, emotional, and spiritual wellness. LOL.

SELF-AWARENESS AND ACCEPTANCE

Our identity, significance, and purpose as believers must be rooted in Christ. Period! We live as impostures when we allow culture, media, peers, personal experiences, and family to determine or shape our identity that does not align with God. We often operate outside of what God says. If we are rooted in truth, it will prevent us from misplacing our identity, significance, and purpose as a child of the Most High King.

When we base our identity on the wrong things rather than God, we travel down a risky path leading to emptiness and insecurity. When we define ourselves solely by external factors such as material possessions, societal approval, personal relationships, or achievements, we build our identity on shifting sands that can easily crumble. True and lasting identity is found in our relationship with God, for He created us in His image, with inherent worth and purpose transcending worldly measures. Only by anchoring our identity in God's love and acceptance can we experience the freedom, fulfillment, and unshakable confidence that comes from embracing our true selves.

Where we place our identity is significant because identity is the foundation for our lives and our well-being. Identity impacts spiritual matters and our pursuit of holiness and Christian maturity. Think about where your identity is rooted. Is it in Jesus or the things of the world? The response to the question makes the difference in how you respond or react to trials and tribulations. It determines how you interact in life. Do you hide parts of yourself to gain acceptance and validation from an ever-judgmental world whose values and beliefs change like the wind? Your response impacts your ability to say "yes" to God's invitation to be your true, authentic, and unique self and continue evolving into the fantastic person He designed you to be.

I tackled the task of searching to see exactly where my identity was rooted. It is and always has been in Jesus. However, I became unfocused because I began to believe the lies the enemy was planting after each ugly encounter with what I thought was love. But because my foundation was strong, I was able to keep standing. I was able to shake off some of the lies that kept me distracted from the truth. It was not enough because I was not dealing with the damaged roots that were working to infect the healthy roots. In this GAP, God has helped me uproot every lie, which has been replaced with His truth. Now when I answer the question, "Who am I?" I have only one response. "I am a child of God." Because of my ability to operate in that truth, I can be all I need to be in my daily roles as a wife, mother, daughter, sister, aunt, friend, entrepreneur, teacher, mentor, and more. Because of my identity, I am established in my position in the Royal Family. I know my character is being changed daily into the likeness of Christ. All that happens in my life is to get me to look more and more imago Dei – ("image of God) or like Christ.

I will repeat it, our identity, significance, and purpose as believers must be rooted in Christ to level up. As I have learned, our identity in Christ must become so ingrained into every aspect of our lives – the very DNA that flows through us is what we need to endure every trial, tribulation, circumstance, and situation that threatens our relationship with Christ. I have learned how important it is to allow DNA to aid me in withstanding a flawed system when it goes against my faith in God and the things I have been taught from His Word.

To be a Christ–follower in today's society, nevertheless, in the legal system, is difficult. Everything stands against the teachings of Christ. The majority want you to conform to their ideas of how you should view yourself while incarcerated. They do and say things to make you feel small and unworthy, less than others. At one point, it caused me great emotional distress until God reminded me of who I am and whose I am. My wholeness, completeness, and identity are not determined by my economic situation, relationship, social status, environment, or positioning. It has everything to do with Jesus and nothing to do with those who view me as less than what my God says I am. Come on, Jesus! No spirit of insecurity residing in this house! I will not allow insecurity or judgmental people to label or identify me. My God has already done it. I trust Him and stand on and operate on what he has said about me and the work He has done in me. I encourage you to take the same stance.

Sidenote: Friends, God looks at our future, but the enemy tries to keep us in our past. God says, "You can, in spite of what has been done," but the enemy says, "You can't because of what you have done." Listen, God will never define you or me by our past issues, mistakes, or missteps, but the enemy will try to confine us by them. I warn you that satan's goal is to keep you chained to the things that draw you away from your authentic identity, whether good, bad, ugly, or indifferent.

Now that should have caused you to come out of the corner. Your energy and life levels just went up. Throw that jab, jab, cross, and return to the ring's middle. It is time to embrace our unique gifts and contribute meaningfully to the world around us.

RECOGNIZING THE SOUL

A Look Inside

Numerous external factors are working against us daily. Many of us are so busy handling or trying to handle the external that we ignore internal factors that hurt our lives. Our mind, for the most part, is an asset, or it could be our greatest enemy. Our mind is the pathway the devil uses to access our lives. The mind can work for us or against us.

We are triune beings. We are spirit, soul, and body. Each component must be handled with care to function to aid us in spiritual growth and holy living. Each part must be connected for us to stand against the enemy effectively. The goal is to keep the spirit high and the flesh low. Matthew 26:41, "Watch and pray, lest you enter into temptation. The spirit indeed is willing, but the flesh is weak." We will examine the soul and its impact when connected or disconnected from the Spirit. The soul is the middleman between the spirit and the flesh.

Spirit -	Soul -	Body
God Connection	Psychological	Temple

The alignment of the spirit, soul, and body is vital to an individual's overall functioning. Each component plays a distinct role in our existence, and when they are in sync. I really need you to understand this principle. It is vital to enhance our ability to remain leveled up each day.

Spirit

> *"I will give you a new heart and put a new spirit within you; I will take the heart of stone out of your flesh and give you a heart of flesh. I will put My Spirit within you and cause you to walk in My statutes and you will keep My judgments and do them"*
> *– Ezekiel 36:26-27 (NKJV).*

The spirit is the divine essence within us. It is the God part of us. It aids us in surpassing our mortal limitations. The spirit is how we can receive God's peace and maintain it. It is where unconditional love, wisdom, and spiritual transformation are powered. Our spirit is what is reborn at new birth. It is immediately saved. The evil nature we are born with is removed, and God gives us His Spirit. We become spiritual beings living a natural experience. Our spirit is perfect, and that is where God resides. Satan does not have access to our spirit. The Spirit's goal is to release the DNA, what I call the (Divine Nature Anointing) of God into our soul. The soul agrees with the spirit and then releases God's DNA to the body. This only happens when the soul agrees with the Spirit. The soul must agree with the Spirit.

Soul

The soul is what makes us unique individuals. It acts as the center of the connection between the spirit and the body, serving as a bridge facilitating communication and unification. Through the soul, the spiritual realm influences our physical experiences and vice versa. It comprises our personality, imaginations, and peculiar internal essence that allows for the expression and manifestation of our deepest desires and aspirations. It is composed of four key factors:

Conscience (moral compass)

Emotion (feelings)

Mind (thoughts)

Will (ambition)

The soul is the portion within us that is not made new at new birth. It is the portion that must be trained and renewed daily for us to function in alignment with the things (requirements) of God. The problem is that many believers do not take the time to train their souls; nevertheless, to seek healing when an injury has occurred. The soul harmonizes the mysterious nature of the spirit with the tangible reality of the body.

The body

The body serves as the vessel through which we experience the sensual aspects of the world. Allowing us to engage with it. The body houses the soul and spirit. To avoid falling into a life driven solely by carnal desires, the body must also be connected to the soul and spirit.

The connection between the spirit, soul, and body serves as a moral compass, enabling the soul to make choices aligned with its true essence of who we are as children of God. The flesh must die so the spirit can have the main role. Remember, what we pour into our souls will determine if the spirit or flesh will rule. As children of God, the spirit must rule.

Lack of Harmony

When circumstances, experiences, and adverse events occur and land a powerful punch to a soul in training or even one trained, it will cause a shift in thoughts and actions and a lack of harmony between the spirit and the soul. We need the true power of faith to assist us with recovering from each blow. A lack of recovery leaves us with internal damage that the devil will gladly use to his advantage. When our souls remain injured, and healing does not take place for whatever reason, it begins to harm our bodies in two ways:

1. become more sensual than spiritual.

2. psychosomatic symptoms manifest in physical form.

I will explain the latter first. A psychosomatic symptom is a clinical term derived from the science of mind and behavior (psychology). Mental and emotional disturbances can become so severe that they manifest as bodily symptoms. For example, someone who is depressed can complain about unexplained body aches. You may go to the doctor with the complaints, and medically – physically – they cannot find anything physically abnormal. That is because the pain is psychological and not physiological. It is in your head. Sounds strange, I know, but

I am trying to help break some overdue yokes. Now you know why the pain reliever does not help with those headaches, backaches, and shoulder and neck pains. These are common pains, but an individual may have more severe issues. My point is that a malfunctioning soul can contribute to a disconnect with the Spirit and cause physical distress.

We all know what happens when we become more sensual than spiritual. It goes beyond sexual immorality. We lose sight of God's purpose and plan for our lives. We lose faith and only believe what we can smell, see, feel, taste, or hear. We become fearful and doubtful of those things we cannot see, smell, touch, taste, and hear. Such functioning impairs our self-confidence, self-control, self-love, and self-esteem. A flawed sense of self can lead to physical and spiritual ruin. A toxic soul must be healed. Jesus is the necessary balm for proper and complete healing.

Untrained Soul

Our soul is primarily made up of our mind, will and emotions, and conscience. Unlike our spirit, the soul was not transformed into the image of Jesus the moment we were born again. Our soul must undergo training to be changed. The power that will train and transform is the Word of God. We must intentionally choose to put God's Word first in our lives every day. Making this intentional decision – God's Word first – brings our conscience, mind, will, and emotions in line with God's will and mind. It changes our thinking, so we increasingly think like He does. We act like He does. We look like Him.

Toxic Soul

A toxic soul has been trained but has strayed due to infection. The seeds of ungodly things have taken root and have contributed to a turf war. This reminds me of a parable Jesus taught, The Wheat and the Tares – Matthew 13:24-29, 36-43. I will paraphrase.

The farmer planted good seeds in his field. The enemy came and planted seeds for weeds once the farmer was asleep. When the plants began to grow, the servants asked the farmer for clarification as to which seed he had planted. The farmer quickly recognized that the enemy tried to ruin his crop. He did not allow his servants to attempt to remove the weeds because the wheat might also be uprooted. He decided to leave them until harvest season. That way, the wheat, and the weeds would be gathered, but the weeds would be removed and destroyed.

What does this have to do with a toxic soul? Well, let me explain. The wheat is the good thoughts that are rooted in God's Word. The weeds are the negative thoughts rooted in the evil planted by the devil and allowed to take root. To clean up the soul – the weeds (negative thoughts) must be uprooted, a thrown out, and God's Word will then take over and continue growing as we plant the right seed.

So many of us have allowed the weeds to stay and pulled up God's. This is why the soul is now polluted and needs to be purged of all toxins immediately. The impurities must be cleaned out starting right now! This is a matter of life and death. Are you reading what I am saying? Right now! How? I got you; you must begin with why you think the way you do. What happened that changed your outlook and perspective? What caused you to see yourself through a dirty lens? Was it some form of abuse (sexual, physical, emotional, or financial)? Were you neglected, rejected, or told you would never amount to anything? Did disappointment due to unmet expectations turn into anger, bitterness, gloom, or despair? What changed you? I will ask the untrained soul what caused your spiritual growth to be stunted. Did you experience ridicule or some form of "Church hurt?" My friends, what seed was planted that changed the trajectory of your focus in life?

Deeper Insight – the Heart

The heart or the inner man is comprised of the spirit and soul. They run so close together that it takes the Word of God to distinguish their differences. Various scriptures tell us to be cognizant regarding matters of the heart. We are to guard our hearts because out of it flows

the issues of life (Proverbs 4:23). We must hide God's Word in our hearts so that we do not sin against Him (Psalms 119:11). Our hearts help us to know how to talk to others and answer questions in love (Proverbs 15:28). What comes from the heart flows out the mouth (Mark 7:21).

My friends, the heart of an unsaved person has a weakened human spirit, having been separated from the life of God. In the nature of every man is an instinctive knowledge of God, even in its weakened state. The soul, which is the place where decisions are made, chooses to listen to the voice of the flesh or the voice of the spirit. In the unsaved, the voice of the flesh speaks loudest because of its weakened nature. The person is carnally minded, sensual, a flesh-led soul.

I will take away your stubborn heart and give you a new heart and a desire to be faithful. You will have only pure thoughts because I will put My Spirit in you and make you eager to obey my laws and teachings (CEV).

However, when the Spirit of God comes into man, he empowers the human spirit, allowing the person to walk in the spirit or be led by the spirit – spirit led. The Spirit of God also opens the Word of God to the believer. The Word purges the soul of false human knowledge and replaces it with God's will and wisdom. When this happens, faith is produced. Hence our ability to level up during the fight. If you are not spiritual or lack orientation to the Spirit, then you will have a problem maintaining and preserving the unity of spirit and soul. It is because your point of reference will be the flesh, not the Spirit of God. Please understand the flesh or body is your human understanding, whereas the Spirit represents God's perspective. The Spirit of God, aka the Holy Spirit, is at work in each believer's life, transforming sin and mending scarred hearts into the image of Christ Jesus.

A poor connection explains why people struggle to overcome emotional injuries and negative thoughts and speak unkind, ungodly, and harsh words to themselves and others. Your spirit and soul have a weak connection and need an adjustment. Our hearts are ready to connect to the soul and do God's will. God has given us the desire and capability to do His will. We must study the Word so that our minds align with our spirits. Hebrews 4:12 states,

> *For the word of God is living and powerful, and sharper than any two-edged sword, piercing even to the division of the soul and spirit, and of joint and marrow, and is a discerner of the thoughts and intents of the heart.*

When we do not take in the Word of God daily, we fail to receive what He has graciously given us to live healthy, whole, and complete. Hence, we continue to walk around broken and unhealed and allow the enemy to control our thoughts. I firmly believe that once we take ownership of our new hearts and train our souls, our healing from past emotional damage will begin to manifest. As we experience new hurts and pains, we will be overcomers and not be pushed to the corner of the ring to be punched and battered by the enemy.

Scriptures of Strength

Ephesians 6:10   Isaiah 43:2

Psalms 119:28   Psalms 46:1

CHAPTER FIVE

REDEDICATE

Life, hardships, and disappointments had left her so defeated. She was no longer rational. Rejection and depression had her so far bound that she no longer knew who she was, nevertheless, her worth. She thought, "What is the point of caring for myself, loving myself more when life is so harsh and cruel and hard? How do I keep going when there is little to no hope or relief?" Sounds familiar? It does to me because she was me.

In recognizing and reconciling my truth, I had to choose to continue down the path I was on or change directions. Make the choice to remain stuck or to move forward. To remain broken or to heal. I had to look past my current circumstance to see life beyond. To be successful, I had to get back to the basics – grab hold of what truly grounds me. I had to reestablish my connection with my foundation – Jesus Christ.

Friends, although we accepted Christ Jesus as our Lord and Savior many moons ago, it may come to a point in our lives when we must reconnect if we have stayed in thoughts, speech, and deeds. You must determine that you will give Christ your all to rise above the turmoil, calamity, and destruction threatening to end your life. To rise above negative thought patterns that produce disconnection, doubt, discomfort, disdain, and death in our souls. That enslaves us to insecurities, infidelity, isolation, and more.

SURRENDERING AND LETTING GO

"Coming to yourself means that you are no longer defined by your circumstances" – Bishop T.D. Jakes.

Confessing sin, repenting, and asking for forgiveness hold profound importance as we rededicate our lives back to Christ and embark on a journey of surrender and letting go of painful events from our past. By acknowledging our sins and shortcomings, we humble ourselves before God, recognizing our need for His forgiveness and grace. Confession becomes a powerful act of surrender as we lay our burdens at the feet of Jesus, releasing the weight of guilt and shame that may have haunted us for far too long.

In the process of rededication, confession paves the way for spiritual renewal and transformation. As we bring our sins into the light, we invite the cleansing power of God's love to wash over us, purifying our hearts and renewing our spirits. Confession enables us to break free from the chains of our past, letting go of the pain and mistakes that may have held us captive. Through this act of confession, we open ourselves up to receive the fullness of God's forgiveness, restoration, and healing. With a contrite heart, we surrender our brokenness to Christ, allowing Him to shape us into vessels of His love, mercy, and redemption.

I gave my life back to Christ and all my brokenness – the shattered and sharded pieces that were my life. I knew that for me to live, I had to die. Not a physical death, but I had to die to the person sin had begun to turn me into. I had to release the desires that caused me to be drawn to worldly thinking and reconnect with my Savior. I let go of what people were saying about me and allowed God's Word to consume my thoughts.

Check this out, God was already ahead of me and created the path to give me the time and space. After being detained for approximately two months, I was told to turn in my orange uniform shirts and given green ones. No one explained what they were for. Over time I understood the original meaning of the color, yet I did allow it to define me. However, treatment was now different. I could no longer walk out of the pod with a pass like those in orange shirts. I had to be escorted. I picked up on the fact that I could not have a cellmate. I had to be isolated from everyone else when I was transported to court.

At first, I was upset. I did not understand why the administration would treat me in such a way. What had I done to be treated in such a manner? It went so far that I was told I could not be on recreational time with everyone else. I became a threat suddenly. But why? I fought against the isolation on rec and won with the help of the psychiatric DNP. Over time I got used to being the only one in green. God allowed me to change my perspective regarding the matter. God gave me His definition because the administration never came to explain the change. I had been set apart. He needed me to be completely alone so that I could focus on the work He was preparing me for. He needed me alone without distractions from a cellmate or multiple cellmates whose spirits would not align with His or mine.

So, when people asked me why I wore green, I told them, "I am set apart, or I am special." When I needed to go to medical or somewhere else in the building, I asked for my security escort because I needed my protection. I changed my perspective, allowing God's purpose to prevail, not man's.

I learned to surrender everything in my rededication process. Rededication is about turning your entire life over to Christ. That means the good and the bad. The ugly and the pretty. Everything! I had to let go of what I wanted to take hold of what God had provisioned for me. I had to surrender what I thought my life should look like for what God had planned. This was not easy because with surrender comes loss. With loss comes grief. However, with grief comes a Comforter. I gained knowledge of who God is and how He presents Himself in my life. I came to a determination to agree with Him and be dependent upon Him.

A KNOWING

When we practice faith in the minors of life, we demonstrate a knowing. This knowing supersedes what we see with our natural vision and what we comprehend with our natural thought process. This knowing is a spiritual awareness. A deep seeded fact that says, "I know God can and He will." We learn to lean on that knowledge because it keeps us hopeful. It provides the water to the seeds of the promise of God's Word that we hold in our hearts. It is a confidence in God that you cannot explain, yet it is there, alive, active, and powerful. An assurance that God cannot fail and that what He has told you is true and will manifest in your life. That knowing keeps hope alive. That knowing keeps faith alive and moving. Knowing increases faith strength each time one of God's promises manifests in your life, or you see Him working on your behalf. Now that I know God for myself, I have moved from the fan club to active teammate status. When we demonstrate consistent faith and obedience, we become committed teammates not just fan club members.

AGREEMENT

Knowing God forms the basis for agreement with Him. We as believers, Christ-followers, must come to a point of agreement where we understand who He is, who we are in relation to Him, and what He requires of us. We must learn what all this means and apply it to the spiritual fight daily. We must choose to come into total agreement with God for faith to perform at full capacity in our lives. Faith makes the difference between a changed or unchanged life. Faith makes the difference between being wholly healed or partially healed or not.

We, as believers, say we believe in God and trust Him. That is until life throws mighty blows and drops "the people's elbow" and "stone-cold stunner" on us. We believe in God until there is some form of lack. If the account is plentiful and all the bills are paid, all is well with our souls. We trust God and believe in Him until sickness occurs. Or believe in God until a loved one dies. Many say they trust God until they

must choose between doing what is correct or potential termination. Many believers claim to have faith in God until the things we value are threatened to no longer be a part of our lives. In these moments, we will be able to see if we truly trust God. In these moments, our alliance is brought to light and tested.

FYI, just because you attended church with Moses or stepped foot inside the church doors every time they open, that does not mean you have come into full agreement with God. Many believers attend church for years and never agree with God. Many try to play "let's make a deal" and come to God on their terms instead of His. No, ma'am, press ham; it does not work that way.

One spiritual weapon that aided me in strengthening my relationship with God and fostering spiritual growth through fellowship is fasting. By setting aside the body's physical needs and praying and seeking God's presence, fasting allowed me to draw closer to Him, gaining a more profound understanding of His character and will. This intentional act of self-denial created an atmosphere of divine communion, where I experienced a heightened sensitivity to God's voice and cultivated intimacy with Him, and I must admit it is a beautiful experience. Friends, fasting developed my knowing and my no. I gained the ability to know God more and say no to what caused me to be out of alignment with Him.

Oh, and just so you will know. When you begin to agree with God, you connect with His peace – that peace that surpasses all understanding (Philippians 4:7). I know because I have experienced it every day since I decided to be intentional in my walk with Christ. This GAP season has not been easy by any means, but the peace Christ gave me is worth more than the enemy could ever offer. I often say, "Now that I have the peace of God, I dare not give it away by entertaining frivolous and niggling acts by others. My Daddy gave this to me, and nothing and no one can take it or have it. If you want your own go to Him and get it. Period!

Agreeing with Abba also causes a peace treaty to form within us – peace of mind (soul) and peace of heart (spirit), an essential connection. The agreement will also strengthen our relationships – God, self, and others. We can live in peace with one another, which is a command. As our knowledge of scripture increases, so does our faith. Come on, Jesus! As faith grows, our agreement with God should as well. I encourage each of you to be intentional in getting to know God and coming into full agreement with Him. Do not say Amen just to be saying it. Say it and mean it, then live the Word you agree with.

DEPENDENCE

When we know God and agree with Him, all that is left to do is to depend on Him. For all the independent folks, let me help you change your life. You are not as independent as you may believe. You also are not "self-made." You have allowed the devil to lie to you long enough. If you were truly independent, you would not be afraid to talk but Jesus on your job out of fear of losing it. You would not have to fear stepping out on faith and starting your own business. We all depend on something or somebody. I encourage you to rely on Him, who created you and our world.

For you to have the ability to live in abundance and provisions of God, you need to rely on the support of God. Many believe their education, skillset, charm, or talents got them the job. Please know that God does the qualifying. He will allow the unqualified to obtain a position where they lack the skillset, then provide on-the-job training. You are not self-made. God made you. God provided the resources so you can make a decent income, drive that car, live in the house, etc. He is our Source, not our resource. He is the reason we cannot just be successful but thrive.

Now that that is out of the way, shall we proceed? Before we (as blood-bought born-again believers) truly develop a functional dependence on our Redeemer, we often must be broken by Him. Why? We get the big head once sin takes over. We believe we are "independent" and "self-made" and that we make moves in our lives that keep us on top. We are sadly mistaken. This is why Hebrews 12:4 must be brought to our attention.

You have not yet struggled to the point of shedding blood in your striving against sin (AMP).

Let's be honest. Some of us continue to sin because we have yet to hit that brick wall that knocks us down so hard and causes us to break that only God can pick us up from. No other help will do. Pride is a sin. When we leave God out of the equation and believe we don't need Him or anyone else, we are filled with sinful pride, and there is a price to pay for such a mindset.

Pick me; I hit that brick wall. What was still intact shattered, God and God alone is the One who not only had to pick me up, but He dusted me off, washed me, performed surgery to mend my brokenness, and cared for me in the recovery room. He is the only One who can get me out of this predicament and restore my physical freedom. My freedom is not to be determined by man. In my brokenness, I became dependent on God. I began to walk out Proverbs 3:5-6, and I will continue. Not just in this test but for the rest of my life. Why? Because my blood has spilled, and I want nothing else to do with sinful living. It is not worth the cost. At 40 years old, I changed my status to dependent. God can file me on His taxes. I depend on Him for everything, in every situation.

I must admit dependence does not come without some form of struggle. The struggle occurs because when the Lord points out the issue, the person, place, possession, pleasure, passion, problem, or habit hindering what He is trying to accomplish in and through us, we buck depending on what He reveals. It can be something as simple as our attitude or habit. It could be a relationship or a place we frequent a lot. It is usually something we have placed over God, and it stands between Him and us. Do we believe Him enough to reposition that relationship, to change that habit or attitude to put Him first and to please Him and not self or man?

Rededicating one's life back to Christ after straying from a life of holiness holds profound importance. It signifies a sincere acknowledgment of our need for God's grace, forgiveness, and restoration. Straying from a life of holiness may result from various factors such as temptation, complacency, or even deliberate rebellion. However, rededication of your life demonstrates a sincere desire to return to the path of righteousness and reestablish a personal relationship with Christ. It symbolizes humility, repentance, and a willingness to surrender our will to God's perfect plan. Rededication is a powerful reminder that God's love is ever-present, ready to embrace and restore those who seek Him. It brings renewed spiritual vitality, a more profound sense of purpose, and a commitment to obedience to God's commandments. By rededicating my life to Christ during the fight, I experienced the transformative power of His grace, found forgiveness, restoration, and the joy of walking closely with Him once again – a sense of knowing. You can have the same experience. It is not too late as long as you have breath. Remember, God's faithfulness is not overcome by our faithlessness, however great it may be. Don't allow satan and his imps to deter you from reconnecting to Christ. God is bigger than your poor judgments, mistakes, and the problems you face. He is for you and me. We must accept His grace, seek forgiveness, and get back into our relationship with Him.

GOD HAS A PLAN

"I know the plans I have in mind for you, declares the LORD; they are plans for peace, not disaster, to give you a future filled with hope" – Jeremiah 29:11 CEB.

GOD'S PLAN

God has a unique and purposeful plan for each believer's life, intricately designed to fulfill His greater kingdom agenda. In this GAP season, circumstances beyond my comprehension leave me questioning and wondering about God's plan for my life. I realized that my understanding is limited, but God's wisdom and knowledge are infinite. Although I cannot ascertain the reasons for the events and challenges in this season and other seasons, I am still responsible for trusting God. I must trust that He has a purpose for everything that has happened.

I have decided to surrender my way, my will, and my lack of understanding and trust in God's plan. Aligning with His will allows me to experience His guidance, provision, and blessings. Believing that with God, nothing is impossible (Luke 1:37). In the moments of surrender, my friends, you and I find strength and power, knowing that we are not alone in our journey toward healing and renewal. We position ourselves to walk in obedience, trust, and faith, knowing that His ways are higher, His wisdom surpasses our own, and His plan leads to the abundant life He desires for us. God's plan exceeds anything you and I can imagine. Even in adversity, we can find hope and inspiration by knowing God is in control. Remember, every setback is an opportunity for a powerful comeback, and every closed door redirects to something better. Trusting in God's plan means His timing is perfect, and His ways are higher than ours.

GOD'S TIMING

God's plan is intricately woven with His perfect timing, orchestrating events and aligning circumstances according to His divine wisdom and purpose. While we may have our own desires and timelines, surrendering our timetable to His will is of utmost importance. It requires us to acknowledge that God's perspective surpasses our finite understanding and that His timing is always for our ultimate good. When we surrender our plans and submit to His timing, we trust His sovereignty and faithfulness. We acknowledge that His ways are higher than ours, and His thoughts are higher than ours.

I can admit that surrendering to God's timetable while incarcerated was difficult for me. In offering my timetable to God, I opened myself up to His transformative work in my life. I released the burden of control and invited Him to guide my path, knowing His plans were far greater and more fulfilling than anything I could imagine or conceive. Surrendering to God's timing cultivated patience, perseverance, and a deeper dependence on Him. It taught me to trust His faithfulness, even when waiting was long and challenging. As I surrendered my timetable, I became more attuned to His leadership, allowing Him to shape my character, refine my faith, and prepare me for the blessings and purposes He has planned. Ultimately, in surrendering to God's perfect timing, I experienced the peace, joy, and fulfillment that comes from walking in alignment with His will.

My friends, I encourage you to let go of the need to understand every aspect or detail of your current predicament or God's will. Take a step forward to grip the power of faith and trust. Believe that your challenges develop you into the person God created you to be. Open your heart and keep your eyes fixed on the goodness ahead. For we know that all things work for the good of those who love God and who are called according to His purpose (Romans 8:28). God has a plan to prosper you and to give you hope and a future (Jeremiah 29:11). Even if it does not seem like it or feel like it right now. I encourage you to start or keep trusting Him. Even amid hardship, His plan is unfolding, filled with blessings and purpose. Embrace it with the confidence that God's love and guidance will never fail you. What the enemy meant for evil, God has worked it out for your good. It may be ugly right now, but God will use it for good. Surrender all to Him right now and watch Him do a good thing. Deliver a powerful right hook to the enemy and rock his world when you surrender your current predicament, past pain, timetable, and life to God.

Scriptures of Strength

2 Timothy 1:7 Psalms 59:16

Psalms 18:1-2 Psalms 118:14

CHAPTER SIX

RELINQUISH

My friends, it is time to level up by letting go of the things that keep you bound. Relinquishing past pain is a courageous and transformative act of self-liberation. It involves consciously letting go of emotional baggage and wounds that have held us captive, allowing us to move forward with greater peace, a sense of self, and freedom. To relinquish past pain, we must first acknowledge and validate our emotions, allowing us to feel and process the pain. Friends, it is imperative that we feel-deal-heal. This can be done through reflection, therapy, coaching, and other healing modalities. By relinquishing emotional baggage, we choose to confront and embrace our pain. We create an opportunity for healing and growth.

The process of letting go involves making a choice to forgive others and ourselves. Forgiveness does not mean condoning the actions that caused the pain but instead exercising our right to express Biblical love and freeing ourselves from the burden of carrying that pain. It is a gift we give ourselves, allowing us to reclaim our power and emotional well-being. Letting go also requires practicing self-compassion and treating ourselves with kindness and understanding. We can choose to release the negative self-talk and self-blame associated with past pain, embracing a narrative of self-love and acceptance. By relinquishing past pain, we open ourselves to new possibilities, personal growth, and the ability to create a future filled with joy, peace, and fulfillment.

UNDERSTANDING MENTAL STRONGHOLDS

"For the weapons of our warfare are not carnal but mighty in God for pulling down strongholds." – 2 Corinthians 10:4.

Mental strongholds are thoughts, arguments, opinions, and beliefs blocking our ability to receive the truth. They grip our minds and influence our behavior, perception of God, self, others, and the world. Strongholds keep us tapped into a self-sabotaging state – rooted in negative or self-limiting thoughts, emotions, experiences, and ways of reasoning that resist the truth.

Strongholds are built in our minds. Through lies and manipulation, the devil sets up strongholds to keep us in the dark. He uses the struggles and sufferings of life to gain access while we are vulnerable. Remember his M.O. from Chapter One? Think about it. What happens when we are the most emotionally, financially, physically, and spiritually vulnerable? We begin to struggle with what is true and what is not. Our mental stability is impaired. When the struggle bus pulls up, we are on it because we fail to be alert to the enemy's workings. We are not paying attention. Not entirely focused on the things of God, and that is when the devil establishes strongholds – through the thoughts we have in those emotionally sensitive and mentally challenging moments and experiences. Until the lie is torn down and the truth of God's Word is established, we will continue to hold onto what is killing us. We will continue to carry emotional baggage from one place to another as we ride the struggle bus.

Mental strongholds are characterized by their ability to distort our perception of reality and reinforce harmful patterns of thought and behavior. They can create barriers to spiritual and personal growth, hinder our ability to make positive changes and limit our potential. Mental strongholds often manifest as self-defeating thoughts, persistent doubts, irrational fears, or deeply ingrained negative beliefs about God, self, and others. Pain is often the catalyst for the formation of these forts.

Painful experiences can lead to feelings of unworthiness, guilt, or shame, causing us to question our inherent value and worthiness of love and connection. These negative thought patterns and beliefs can hinder our spiritual and personal growth, preventing us from experiencing the fullness of divine love and wisdom and a life of abundance. Mental strongholds rooted in pain can limit our ability to trust in the divine plan, cultivate faith, and contribute to our surrender to the flow of life's experiences.

When we actively address and dismantle mental strongholds, we create space for personal and spiritual awareness, development, and growth. By recognizing healing, the wounds that gave rise to these strongholds, we open ourselves up to a deeper connection with God. As we release self-limiting beliefs and embrace self-compassion and love, we can explain our spiritual awareness and cultivate personal development, which incites a greater sense of inner peace, purpose, and alignment with the person God designed you and me to be. We embark on a transformative spiritual journey that allows us to reconnect with our Heavenly Father and experience profound spiritual growth.

EMOTIONAL WOUNDS

Painful experiences can create deep emotional wounds that give rise to negative thought patterns and beliefs that shape our perception of God, ourselves, and the world around us. When left unaddressed or unhealed, these wounds contribute to the establishment of mental strongholds and negative personality traits that keep us bound and hinder our personal and spiritual growth, development, and relationships with others. It is vitally necessary to get to the root of our issues to break the yokes that bind us to the things outside of God's will and those that block us from being the person God designed us to be. Nevertheless, the blessings that come with obedience-holy living. Many of us carry around baggage that contains past hurt and fear. We walk around damaged emotionally because we either don't know we are hurt or fail to address the damage because we are afraid to reveal our pain to others. We are in denial, and it is easier to function in dysfunction because you know what to expect.

I remember changing the name of my private practice to The Root Behavioral Health. I recognized the importance of dealing with root issues. My aim was to aid my clients in moving beyond the surface to deal with the primary source of their identified problem (s). The reason for their distress. During my own process of healing, I listened to the teachings of Dr. Tony Evans whenever I could. I recall him saying in many sermons that we must deal with the root rather than the fruit if we want things to turn around. I would shout many "Amens" and "What you said" in agreement with him.

Emotional wounds are a result of an offense that took place that was not addressed. Unresolved pain is derived from offenses we fail to address promptly. These things contribute to a change in our perspective on life and even core beliefs. Things such as trauma from sexual, physical, or emotional abuse, neglect, rejection, toxic statements, being lied to or cheated on, divorce, loss of a loved one, loss of a job or friendship, etc. These things changed the trajectory of our lives, causing us to view people, places, and possessions in a different light. Usually, a negative one. Emotional wounds are deep hurts that we have yet to heal from and can't shake, yet they shape the course of our lives. Emotional injuries impact how we show up in life. How we view the world around us. How we treat others and ourselves. Many with unhealed emotional wounds compromise values and integrity and become blind to their worth. They question their existence and set goals based on a flawed view of self and life.

It is time to identify corrupt seeds and address the root damage. The source cannot be uprooted, but that which comes from it can. We do not have to leave damaged roots in the soil of our hearts and souls. God has equipped us with tools to pull up tainted roots and plant seed that grows roots of love and produce fruit of patience, joy, peace, and more. My friends, the seed of trauma was planted. The origins of pain and fear produced the fruit of doubt, lack of trust, toxic thoughts, anger, resentment, aggressive behavior, mean and nasty attitude, etc. The damaged roots must go so that something new and healthy can take their place. This is where the Word of God comes into play. We must plant a new seed – the Word and grow new roots and produce fresh fruit.

Three categories of emotional damage contribute to strongholds that must be considered and dealt with as they apply to our lives. Remember, the longer we remain in an injured state of being, the more susceptible we are to fall on the ropes or being pinned in the corner and the devil taking advantage, causing more damage. Since we are in a fight, think of strongholds as the broken ribs, bloody nose, swollen eye, or concussion some sustain in a boxing match. Barriers that keep you from performing at your best or making progress. They give the opposition an advantage and can cost you the fight.

Three Categories of Emotional Damage

1.Past damage: This group consists of the many things we want to avoid thinking about, talking about, or dealing with. Things include trauma, abuse, neglect, lack of love, companionship, esteem, or acceptance. Choices in teen years and adulthood that have triggered difficult consequences and deep regret. Unconfessed or exposed sin, mistakes, missteps, and mishaps you still feel guilty and ashamed about. Heartbreak and heartache from toxic relationships.

2.Present damage: The here and now. Things we deal with directly that contribute to emotional injury. The trials, tribulations, and tests we face currently cause us spiritual and emotional distress and fatigue. Relationships -marital, parent-child, friendships, family problems, work-related issues, impulsive reactions, health issues, financial problems, and any other lack, attack emotional stability. Such instability makes you look for comfort food, illicit relationships, drugs, alcohol, gambling, and any quick fix to distract or numb, which can lead to even more damage. Unhealed emotional injury can contribute to doubting God's love, protection, and provision.

3.<u>Future damage</u>: This group deals with foreboding. Damage is caused by worrying about what could possibly happen. Anxiety that causes you to be paralyzed in the here and now. Robbing you of peace and joy.

Some individuals may fit into one or two categories, and some all three. The good news is you can be loosed from all. It is a choice you must make. We must let go of the offenses from the past we have brought into our present. The past pain mixed with the current pain keeps healing from taking place. Prolonged healing of emotional wounds must be dealt with ASAP. Past pain becomes a nemesis to the present. Each offense we encounter must be dealt with swiftly. Compound or accumulated offenses are detrimental to our emotional and mental stability. Unaddressed accumulated offenses contribute to fortified strongholds that can lead to breakdowns in our emotional and mental well-being. We must identify the source, isolate the lies, replace them with God's truth, and be healed and set free. Put some truth-God's Word, on it!

DEFEATING STRONGHOLDS

The weapons of our warfare are not carnal, but mighty through God to the pulling down of strongholds – 2 Corinthians 10:4

We are in an ongoing spiritual war. During the war, we engage in various fights- some minor and some major. We must accept that dealing with the inner self is vital when dismantling emotional strongholds. It requires embracing vulnerability, self-reflection, and a willingness to explore and confront deep-seated beliefs, wounds, and patterns of thought that contribute to the stronghold's grip. Each trial, tribulation, storm, problem, situation, adversity, and predicament is a battle in and of itself. How we endure each fight impacts our functioning in daily life. We must acknowledge that our mind is the battlefield. We must gain control by connecting our soul to our spirit to fight in the proper realm and the right enemy with the correct weapons. In this GAP season, my fight is fought in the boxing ring of my mind.

I understand that mental strongholds are the work of spiritual forces that seek to undermine my faith and distort my perception of the divine truth. Ephesians 6:12 states, "For our struggle is not against flesh and blood, but against the rulers, against the authorities, against the powers of this dark world and against the spiritual forces of evil in the heavenly realm." These forces can use pain to sow seeds of doubt, fear, and negativity in our minds, leading to mental strongholds that keep us captive. Satan and his imps are the forces that we must fight against.

The Bible offers guidance and hope for breaking free from mental strongholds. Second Corinthians 10:4 says, "For the weapons of our warfare are not carnal, but mighty through God to the pulling down of strongholds." The weapons we fight with are not weapons from the world. In this fighting environment, we have the divine power to demolish strongholds. "We demolish arguments and every pretension that sets itself up against the knowledge of God, and we take captive every thought and make it obedient to Christ" (v5). Through the power of God, we can overcome these mental strongholds. By aligning our thoughts and core beliefs with the truth of God's Word, practicing spiritual disciplines such as prayer and meditation, and seeking guidance from the Holy Spirit, we can dismantle these strongholds and experience spiritual freedom and growth. Trust me, I am a living witness.

TACTICAL STRATEGIES

A significant part of breaking loose from and pulling down strongholds that exalt themselves above the knowledge of God is dealing with beliefs and thoughts that oppose God. Convictions and ideas that are toxic and block us from living healthy, godly lives. To level up over strongholds set up by the evil one, we must take wrong beliefs and thoughts captive to the obedience of Christ.

Changing Core Beliefs

Changing core beliefs not aligning with God's Word is paramount for emotional, mental, and spiritual well-being and living purpose-driven lives. Flawed core beliefs can hinder progress, limit potential, and contribute to self-sabotaging behavior patterns. When considering changing core beliefs, it is crucial to approach the process with intentionality. We must make a deliberate effort to challenge and replace these negative or flawed beliefs with positive, empowering ones that align with God's Word. This can be achieved through self-reflection, self-analysis, and working with a trusted individual or professionals. The key is recognizing the origin and impact of flawed beliefs, developing alternative perspectives, and reframing distorted thinking. To aid me in shifting negative thoughts and cultivating new and healthier views and perspectives, I engaged in practices such as meditation - mindfulness, positive affirmations, self-compassion, and spiritual activities. Friends, changing core beliefs is a process that requires patience, perseverance, positivity, and commitment to personal development and spiritual growth. The transformative impact it will have on your life will be invaluable. I am experiencing the transformation, so I know.

Friends, the devil wants to infiltrate your belief system. He wants to influence what you believe is true about God, yourself, and the things you experience. He knows that if he can change your beliefs, he can change your character. By changing your character, he can change your actions. Resulting in changing what you believe is possible. Remember, for with God, nothing is impossible (Luke 1:37). As believers, our identity is in God, but if the enemy has a say, he will do all he can to cause us to forget or to think differently.

CHANGING THOUGHT PATTERNS

Casting down imaginations, and every high thing that exalted itself against the knowledge of God and bringing into captivity every thought to the obedience of Christ -2 Corinthians 10:5 (KJV).

This verse clearly states for us to throw out, dismiss, and ignore every thought that comes against what we know to be true about the things of God. If we do not do it, the devil will catch us slipping. He will use whatever vulnerable moment or experience he can to get us to fear or doubt or be misinformed. In doing so, we second-guess ourselves and God and operate based on incorrect information. The stronghold is being built. The more we doubt, fear, or act out of ignorance, the stronger and more extensive the fort becomes. Eventually, we fall or stray. The beautiful thing about God is that even when we go off the beacon path or fall, He will redirect us, pick us up, dust us off, and love us. I feel a shout coming! I know He will do it for you because He did it for me and is doing it for me. Proverbs 24:16a (NIV) states, "For though the righteous fall seven times, they rise again."

Secondly, we must do as Romans 12:2 instructs us, "Be not conformed to this world: but be ye transformed by the renewing of your mind, that ye may prove what is that good, and acceptable, and perfect, will of God"- (KJV). Friends, we must eliminate every toxic thought that undermines what God has spoken to you regarding who you are and what plans He has for you. Every thought that exalts itself against Christ and keeps you bound to negativity, pain, and suffering must be relinquished. Every thought that stops forward progression must be eradicated.

Thirdly, we must replace wrong thoughts with those based on God's Word. Always remember that one of satan's strategies is to plant unhealthy thoughts in your mind, repeating them over and over until you start to think they are your own thoughts. I often tell my Aunt GMC, "You got to put some truth on it." This means putting the truth of God's Word up against the negative thoughts the enemy has suggested or planted. This is not a one-and-done method. We must practice this principle every day. The mind determines if we elevate our faith, hope, and trust in God to a point where trouble doesn't weigh us down or take us out. We must have a made-up mind to trust God's Word. Placing the Truth on the situation will lift us in times of trouble. God becomes our stronghold. Faith is essential for this method to be effective. This confidence is built in the heart. Faith comes by hearing and hearing by the Word of God (Romans 10:17).

Please read this slowly. If your thinking is not right, your words won't be right, and eventually, your behavior won't be proper. When we identify flawed beliefs and wrong thinking, we must be willing to rid ourselves of them at all costs and replace them with God's thoughts. The more we do this, it will take root and become a habit which is an automatic response. I had to put this into practice to align my beliefs and thinking with the Word to overcome those distortions, distractions, and demons. Now, I can reject wrong thoughts before they take root. My thought patterns changed. I see my struggles from a different perspective and handle them differently. I no longer view this GAP season as a curse but a blessing because it has not defined me but allowed me to be refined. It has given me the power to level up. Now I can speak like David and say,

"God is my refuge and strength, a very present help in trouble" – Psalm 46:1 (personalization).

"The Lord is my rock and my fortress, and my deliverer; my God, my strength, in whom I will trust; my buckler and the horn of my salvation, and my high tower" - Psalm 18:2 (KJV).

Friends, please be mindful of the devil. Do not let him have free reign in your mind. Turn to God and allow Him to be your refuge and strength.

Changing Control

Relinquishing the grip of control and surrendering to God is a life-changing act that paves the way for embracing healing. Our ability to recognize the limitations of our own power and humbly yield to God places us in a position to be loosed from the things that hold us, hostage. By relinquishing control to God, we entrust our deepest hurts and scars into His hands, accepting that there is a purpose and a plan beyond our understanding. Believing that all things work for the good of those who love Him and are called according to His purpose. In the surrender, we find solace and a renewed sense of hope as God's omnipotent and compassionate nature gently guides us toward healing. As we let go, our burdens become lighter, and the wounds that once defined us begin to lose their grip on our souls. Through unconditional surrender, we open ourselves to divine grace and mercy, allowing the soothing balm of God's divine love to permeate every crevice of our wounded hearts. In shifting control from us to God, we discover the transformative power of surrender and experience the profound freedom of letting go of control to Him, who has all power, is ever present, and all-knowing.

BE REAL

It is time, to be honest about the pain you carry. The fear you harbor. One or both are keeping you from being healthy in your soul. The lack of honesty allows satan to use your pain to establish strongholds in your mind. Being honest comes with being willing to be truthful, vulnerable, and open with God and yourself. It requires you to get out of your own way. By doing so, the portal to healing will open. Being honest with yourself permits you to get to know yourself as you feel-deal-heal. Being honest with God allows you to rebuild your relationship with Him as you demonstrate your desire to reconnect by releasing your truth to Him and being obedient to His Truth. You will also receive strength and wisdom to deal with the unlovely parts of yourself.

Being real with self is a challenging feat. I had to dig deep because of the thick walls and barriers of defense methods. I had to go beyond the surface because my strongholds began to be built in my childhood, and I did not recognize this truth until this GAP season. I had to get to the nitty gritty because of the path pain led me down unknowingly. Acknowledging that even when the sting of the pain is gone, it can still direct the course of your life when the injury remains unaddressed. The infection develops and works its way into your personality, character, and every crevice of your life. It is a silent killer.

A change of direction was necessary to break the chains. To be loosed from the strongholds that held me hostage. The tricky part was not the uncovering, although it was like ripping off a band-aid to reveal the injury. The hard part was accepting. I had to examine, with God's help, the severity of the injury and infection. It left me vulnerable and very exposed. I was uncomfortable. I had to accept that I was damaged and needed help to heal and recover. In accepting my truth, I struggled with the "why?" Why did God allow this? Why did God choose now to expose me? Why did it have to be this extreme and public?

Nonetheless, my secret was exposed, my wounds were open, and I had to be attended to. I had to confront the damage without professional or spiritual guidance. I could talk to family and friends, but not about the more profound things I was dealing with. My faithful and only source of help was God and God alone.

Friends, in my GAP, I had a come-to-Jesus meeting, and I had to make a decision. I had to decide whether to be loosed or to stay bound. To remain laid out on the canvas waiting for the final count or rise, stand firm, and be steadfast, immovable. To be free in the LORD or be bound by my past sins, mistakes, and mess-ups. To believe God's thoughts of me or be defined by the world's judgmental thoughts and opinions. So, I chose to rededicate my life back to Jesus. After rendering my answer, the work began, and hear me when I tell you (in my husband's voice) it was not an easy task. However, I embraced the journey because I did not want to continue to see myself out of broken pieces. I no longer wanted to be damaged or live an injured life. I no longer wanted to cause unintentional pain to those I loved and others. Sinful, broken living was not and is not God's plan for my life. So, I did the work with God's help. I encourage you to do the same. Strongholds established by the evil one can be broken. Are you willing to do the work? The beauty is you don't have to do it alone. God has given me to you through this book to aid you.

FEEL-DEAL-HEAL PROCESS

Steps to Feel-Deal-Heal

My most famous therapeutic phrase is feel-deal-heal. It is vital in overcoming and moving forward. It is necessary for becoming the person God designed you and me to be. Recovery requires work. Healing must take place to regain health, balance, and stability to level up. You must put in the work. When I say feel-deal-heal, I am encouraging you to do the following:

1. Acknowledge the seed– the incident, words spoken, what was done to cause you pain or caused you to fear.

2. Feel the emotions attached to the situation.

3. Deal with the beliefs and thoughts derived from the situation. Replace unhealthy with healthy.

4. Heal- accept and move forward by faith.

Got it? In the dealing, we address the toxic waste, including triggers, and set a plan for overcoming it until complete healing occurs. The aim is to work hard to acknowledge the flawed beliefs, triggers, and strongholds and put God's Truth on them to set healing in motion. Until total healing comes, we learn to address and remove stingers to ease the pain quickly. Do not allow an offense to go unaddressed. Healing is a process. Healing requires us to do our part and allow God to do His.

If we fail to heal, we fail to receive the peace of God, which passeth all understanding (see Philippians 4:7). Emotional injuries get in the way of us living a life of abundance according to the provisions Abba has established for each of us. They keep us standing in our own way. Unhealed emotional wounds mean our minds are working against us and not for us. We become partners with the enemy due to a lack of healing.

It is time to power up and throw another powerful jab-cross combination with a solid right hook and an uppercut to get the enemy to back up and give you fifty feet. Are you ready? Great! Let's do this! It's go time! It is time to put in the work. The longer you remain injured, the longer you will be without real power to overcome life's troubles. You remain insecure and feel inferior. The longer you stay injured, the longer you remain indebted to sin and out of God's will. Our thoughts perpetuate the cycle of pain. They cause an otherwise intelligent, calm, self-controlled, competent person to make foolish, ungodly choices, resulting in further emotional damage and spiritual disconnection. Pick me. I got a testimony for that. Our inability to be unbound from evil strongholds keep us from rising to the next level.

I have learned so many things about myself during the GAP and am grateful. Friends, time does not heal emotional wounds. Not allowing someone to help us process those injuries only causes the wounds to grow deeper. A lack of healing contributes to the pain seeping deep into the crevices of our soul and spirit and impacting our personality and even character. Problem after problem. Disappointment after disappointment. Relationship after relationship, pain piles up in our souls and hearts, and we struggle, even bend some break. Why? We can only handle so much. Some can take more than others, but we all come to our breaking point when the infection becomes too severe. I never dealt with the years of accumulated pain until I was forced to in this GAP.

Listen, if the mounds of pain surface simultaneously, you could be in serious trouble. In hindsight, I was in trouble and didn't even know it. Yes, Dr. Daniels did not detect the level of severity of her own pain and suffering. I was too busy caring for others and prioritized myself wrong. During this forced timeout and season of being set apart, I have had time to recognize my level of distress and correct course and

feel – deal – heal. I will tell you this when you have not allowed God to purge and purify you and you meet another individual who is just as impure, the pull from the enemy will be so strong it will consume you before you even know it. That spiritual connection leads to the death of many things, which is not a comfortable experience. It will knock you down, but you don't have to stay down. Rise up and fight!

Scriptures of Strength

John 16:33 Psalms 27:1

Psalms 29:11 Psalms 73:26

CHAPTER SEVEN

RECLAIM

I have two amazing maternal sisters. Being the oldest is a hard job, but Nicole and Denise made it easy – for the most part. I love my bond with my sisters. As we became adults, we began to apply this unspoken rule. Whenever you borrow an item, such as a dish or a shirt, if the owner does not retrieve it within 30 days, it becomes yours. It was funny to hear us debate over who skillet was whose. This included our mother. The pot or pan was usually our mother's, but we took ownership after 30 days. Mother became hip to the game, so she would call to reclaim her items and have us return the pot or pan immediately. It was funny to see her reaction during a gathering when she observed a particular thing she knew was hers. By the end of the night, she reclaimed what was hers most of the time without saying a word.

Once I understood how to develop and grow my faith, I began to reclaim the things the enemy had stolen from me. I am encouraging you to do the same. As you get your stuff back, place it in the Lord's hands for protection and prioritizing.

GET YOUR STUFF BACK

I have identified a few things that are necessary to reclaim as we continue the process of healing and growing. As you continue with the healing process, you may identify other things. Things we must reclaim: 1. Identity 2. Focus 3. Appetite 4. Power.

Identity

Reclaiming your identity begins with spending time with the One who designed you. God knows everything about you, down to the number of hairs on your head. When we spend time with our Creator, we can begin to read His thoughts about us and His plans and provisions for His Children. You may not think that you need to reclaim your identity, but if you wear a mask every day pretending to be okay, and you are not – reclaim. If you present with a façade – reclaim. You have a persona you show up with that demonstrates confidence you truly lack – reclaim. You were once kind and gentle, and now you are mean and aggressive -reclaim. You once walked with integrity and were honest, but now you manipulate and lie – reclaim. It is time to stop living according to the lies the enemy has told you about being "too damaged" and "too far gone." Take back the personality and character that was given to you. Be intentional about demonstrating and growing the fruit of the Spirit – love, joy, peace, faithfulness, kindness, gentleness, meekness, longsuffering, and self-control. I was determined to display at least two each day until they became a habit and eventually became who I am. I would draw the following flower as a reminder. I drew it on everything. I had enough pedals to write the fruit of the Spirit in each - joy, peace, love, faithfulness, gentleness, kindness, humility, longsuffering, and self-control.

Just in case you have been told that you do not matter. That you are not enough. You have been made to feel less than. Please read my following words slowly and out loud. Say to yourself, "I matter!' repeat out loud, "I matter!" You are alive today because God kept you alive. That means you have a great purpose that He has for you to fulfill. I, too, have a calling on my life, and God has shown me that I will remain on this earth until I complete it. My friend, YOU MATTER more than the pain you carry. You MATTER more than the problems, the abuse, the rejection, the lack, etc. YOU MATTER, YOU MATTER, YOU MATTER, YOU MATTER so much that God chose you. Trust me and God, no matter what the enemy has told you or is telling you. You matter.

You are fearfully and wonderfully made – Psalm 139:4

You are more than a conquer – Romans 8:37

You are strong – Isaiah 41:10

You are loved – John 3:16

You are chosen – (you didn't add the scripture.)

I could go on and on. Just hear me when I tell you, YOU MATTER, and trouble don't last always. God gives us a life worth living when we choose to fully agree with Him. We will discuss this a little later.

FOCUS

We must not allow our problems to define us, nor should they blind us. We must keep them from becoming the most significant focus in our lives. We must stop putting the spotlight on a problem to the point it consumes us and causes us to become unstable in our thinking, speech, actions, and perspective.

Unstable: Not mentally or physically balanced. Tending to change. When we become unstable due to focusing more on our problems than anything else, or we believe the lies the enemy is suggesting, our minds become subject to disorder. We lack the substance we need to

be balanced and whole. We become vulnerable to mental diseases or defects because our minds are functioning in an abnormal state. If we are angry all the time – abnormal state. Filled with envy and jealousy – abnormal state. Insecure and lack confidence – abnormal state. Depressed, hopeless – abnormal state. We are not created to remain in an abnormal state as our norm.

I had to change my focus. I was determined to get back to my "normal." It began with a statement, "Stay Kingdom Focused." This statement became my norm. I end my phone calls and letters with it. I say it to encourage others. One day an acquaintance wrote me and asked me to explain "Kingdom focused." My response: "Kingdom-focused is a reminder to keep one's eyes on God and nothing else. Believing God will supply what I need when I need it. Kingdom-focused is keeping the faith. Keeping God first is being kingdom focused. Staying out of the way and not getting caught up in drama and shenanigans is being kingdom focused. All-in-all kingdom focused is a reminder to lead a life set apart for God no matter your positioning, situation, or circumstance." Now that can preach! Come on, Jesus.

Honestly, the question caught me by surprise. I never gave any in-depth thought to the phrase. I started saying it knowing what it meant to me. My family began to repeat it because they knew it was essential to my healing and stability. So, as I continued to ponder more about what "kingdom focused" meant, these are the words I recorded in a letter to my wonderful and amazing husband and best friend: "Bae, God had to purge a lot of toxic waste out of me. The damage was deep, which is why I was so easily manipulated. I am grateful for healing despite my current circumstance. I had to change many core beliefs about how I perceived myself. Now, I can show up without the mask. I can verbalize that I am not good when things are not right in my life. No more defensive mechanisms to hide my truth. Learning to pay attention to my thoughts and putting the Word on those that did not and do not align with God's Word has helped me stay focused. I have learned to be intentional about paying attention to my thoughts. Thoughts jumpstart the daily journey. Anything that goes against what God says must be quickly dismissed. It is a constant, persistent choice we must make. That is why being kingdom focused is more than a saying for me. It is my lifeline. It is how I show obedience and gratitude to God. To glow up is how I choose to show up daily in life."

Set your mind and keep focused habitually on the things above [the heavenly things], not on things that are on the earth [which have only temporal value]
– Colossians 3:2 (AMP)

My friends, for us to "one-up" on the opponent and reclaim our stuff, we must focus on the right things – godly things. Have the proper perspective – a godly perspective. Become habitual in how we move. If our focus is off, we become unstable in our thoughts, speech, and actions, thus causing us to decrease in power. We must always do things God's way. It must not be "second nature" but our primary way of functioning. For that to happen, we must do a few things consistently. Three steps we must take every day:

1. Cast - We must cast down all thoughts that are in contradiction to God's Word. We discussed this in detail in Chapter Two. If you need to go back and review, please do so. It is vital to your upward movement and retrieval of your stuff on the way. Once we rid ourselves of the toxic waste, we have room for the things of God we reclaim. These will help us grow into healthy, beautiful, God-fearing, stable, loving, and healed individuals.

Casting down arguments and every high thing that exalts itself against the knowledge of God, bringing every thought into captivity to the obedience of Christ – 2 Corinthians 10:5.

2. Choose - We must intentionally focus on God's Word and those things of God. Philippians 4:8 gives us a great example of the things to focus on.

...Whatever is true, whatever is honorable and worthy of respect, whatever is right and confirmed by God's Word, whatever is pure and wholesome, whatever is lovely and brings peace, whatever is admirable and of good repute; if there is any excellence, if there is anything worthy of praise, think continually on these things [center your mind on them, and implant them in your heart] (AMP).

There we have it. We do not have to wonder about what to replace our old focus and thoughts with. We have a nice list inside this verse to get us started and keep us going. No more excuses. Be like Nike, and just do it for your sake. For your peace of mind. Remember, this must be a daily and constant choice. Be intentional!

3. Conform - We must practice what we believe. Practice what we have learned. Practice what we speak when it comes to God's Word.

The things which you have learned and received, and heard and seen in Me, practice these things [in daily life], and the God [who is the Source] of peace and well-being will be with you – Philippians 4:9 (AMP)

We must practice obedience by applying God's Word to our daily lives. It will show up in our thoughts, speech, and actions.

APPETITE

Our natural desire to sin must change. Once we are reborn, the blood of Jesus redeems us from the curse of sin. If sin is still a natural craving, we must work to change our appetites – our diet. The appetite (our nature) was changed at the new birth. God gave us a new spirit, but we will not acquire the new taste if we do not alter our diets. Our diet consists of what we consume regularly through conversations, music, television, entertainment, reading, etc. We must acquire a new preference for people, places, possessions, passions, and pleasures and passions that are connected to our new life. We must change our diet to be fit for the next level. Our preference must be for God and the things of God. "We must feast," as my Aunt Gladys often says, "on His Word daily."

I am an athlete. I enjoy playing sports. It keeps me physically and mentally healthy. At one point in high school, I dreamed of playing at the next level in both basketball and volleyball. I desired to earn a scholarship for either or both. That way, I could fulfill three dreams at once. I would have the opportunity to get a higher education, play sports at the college level, and pay for college and not acquire the burden of student loans.

I went to college, but sports did not pay for it. Sadly, I have the burden of student loans. However, I got a chance to play college basketball. It was short-lived. I was a walk-on, but I made the team. The day before the first game, I turned in my gear. Why? It was not the same. It was not fun for me – my appetite had changed. Coach called me into her office. When I explained my reasoning for letting go of my dream she stated, "But you worked so hard to get back in shape. You can do this." I appreciated her encouragement. I did work hard. I had just had my second child right before the fall semester began. I had put in double, triple the work to perform on the next level. I had to cast, choose, and conform each day to prepare for game day.

As believers, we must make a choice. I chose to accept that my preference had changed. I no longer ate, slept, or breathed basketball. I enjoyed changing diapers and having feeding time – being a wife and a mother. My new diet was consistent with things that helped me in my new roles and advanced my family. So, you may believe that I quit, but I am telling you I had a diet change. We, as believers, must change our diets when our appetite changes.

Focus contributes to our ability to make the necessary changes. We must choose pure or profane. God or the enemy. The devil will use whatever he can to squeeze his way into our lives. He will do what

he can to stay if he already has access. At the drafting of this book, I am physically incarcerated. It has been 2.9 years – 33 months – 1014 days at the writing of this chapter. To lose focus would be detrimental. My predicament is complex, and the environment is satan's stomping ground. So, I had to acquire a new taste for God's Word and the things of Him not to be overtaken and indulge in the diet that the majority consume daily in this environment.

Many of the younger and older ladies enjoy reading urban books. It becomes serious if they do not have a new book to read. The complaints are loud and continuous until someone satisfies the "need." Many ladies came to me to talk about the heavy load of incarceration and their walk with God. They ask questions about God's Word and why it does not seem to be helping, or they struggle to change their actions. Some wonder if God is listening to their prayers. Others wonder why they cannot hear God's voice. I tell them, "Change your diet." Sadly, they do not take heed to my advice. They continue to read profane material that feeds the lust of the flesh. Some even have open discussions about unholy things they will engage in upon release. I do not have a judgmental mindset. I pray for them and continue to guide them in the right direction. Friends, what we feed is what will grow.

To complete my basketball story. I moved to Texas after graduating from undergrad. I was divorced by this time. I played pick-up basketball with a few ladies I met at church. It was fun! After one of our games, a gentleman approached me and asked if I was interested in trying out for the WNBA. Say what now? I can still play on the next level. It sounded good, and my love for basketball still existed, but my appetite had changed. I enjoyed being free to parent my fellas. Plus, I was not in shape for trying out for that level of commitment. I liked eating ding dongs and drinking Pepsi. My focus was different. My relationship with my boys meant more to me than anything else then. The impact would be too much on our relationship. Doing things God's way and my fellas were my new flavors.

POWER

When we align our identity, focus, and appetites with God, we reclaim our stuff and gain back our power and authority. Our faith grows because we live a life set apart for God. We begin to see the power of the Holy Spirit rise in us as we practically apply God's Word. Our character changes, our mindsets change, and we crave the things of God. The more we feed on the Word, the better we become to deal with opposition, rejection, insecurity, betrayal, trials, tribulations, death, loss, etc. They teach us instead of tearing us down. We learn to overcome and not be overtaken. We learn to speak the Word during the struggle to rise above it all and have peace that surpasses all understanding. God's super connects with our natural, and we can defy the things working against us in the spirit realm.

REWRITING THE NARRATIVE

Rewriting the narrative after going through a life-changing event requires having a different perspective than you had before. I embraced a spiritual philosophy which became a transformative and empowering process. Friends, healing from emotional injuries is a powerful and liberating process that allows us to reclaim our lives and move forward with renewed strength and resilience. Emotional wounds can stem from various sources, such as trauma, past relationships, negative self-beliefs, or unaddressed accumulated offenses. However, we can rewrite our stories about our experiences, emotions, and self-worth through healing and growth.

The first step in rewriting the narrative is implementing the feel-deal-heal process. Acknowledging and embracing the pain, emotions, and experiences that arise from the life-changing event(s). It is essential to validate and embrace the feelings that arise from dealing with the things that injure us. To grieve, feel the pain, and process the emotions associated with the event. We must cultivate a safe space that allows us to feel-deal-heal. Spirituality provides a container for these experiences and offers a safe space for reflection, prayer, meditation, etc. Through this connection, we can find strength, guidance, and the capacity to make meaning out of our circumstances. This can be done through guided assistance from a therapist, life or spiritual coach, support groups, or self-refection practices such as journaling and meditation. I had to do the latter in this season of my life. Doing so gives us permission to feel and release the pain; we create space for growth and transformation.

Once we have acknowledged our emotional wounds, we can reframe our perspective and beliefs about ourselves and the event. Rather than seeing a situation solely as a source of pain or loss, we can view it as an opportunity for growth, development, and transformation. This involves challenging negative self-perceptions and core beliefs that may have been ingrained because of the emotional damage. By practicing self-compassion and self-acceptance, we can replace self-limiting and self-sabotaging beliefs with empowering ones. The shift in perspective allows us to cultivate resilience and find purpose within the narrative. We can explore questions such as "What lessons can I learn from this experience?" Instead of asking, "Why." We can shift our narrative from one of victimhood to one of flexibility, strength, and growth. Spiritual affirmations, positive self-talk, and engaging in value-adding activities that reinforce our self-worth can support this process.

As we rewrite the narrative, it is vital for us to embrace forgiveness and compassion, both towards ourselves and others involved in the life-changing event. Forgiveness does not mean condoning or forgetting the pain but instead releasing the grip of resentment and allowing ourselves to heal. My definition of forgiveness is "exercising our right to express biblical love when someone has caused you some form of hurt." It involves acknowledging the humanity and imperfections of others, recognizing that we all sin, make mistakes, and face challenges. By extending forgiveness, we free ourselves from the burden of carrying anger and resentment, making space for healing and growth.

As you and I write our narrative, it is crucial to cultivate spiritual and self-care practices that nurture our emotional well-being and inner peace. Practices that develop us both spiritually and personally. Engaging in activities that bring us peace and joy, practicing self-compassion, setting boundaries (spiritual and personal), and prioritizing our spiritual, mental, emotional, and physical health are essential components of the healing process. By creating a nurturing environment that supports our spiritual and personal growth, we foster a sense of self-love and reinforce a new narrative we are making that aligns with God's Word.

Each day I am intentional about having my one-on-one time with Jesus – 15-30 minutes of prayer, reading the word, meditation, praise, and worship. It is vital to my overall health. I like doing it first thing in the morning to start my day on a godly beat. I also have a song of the day that helps me shift my mood if something unfavorable happens externally or keeps me focused on positive, divine things. I intentionally write down at least three things I am grateful for, followed by three powerful I AM statements.

Additionally, having a robust and healthy support system, such as a therapist, counselor, coach, or trusted family and friends, can be instrumental in rewriting the narrative after healing from emotional injuries. The ability to have a safe place to share our experiences and vulnerabilities with others who can be trusted and offer understanding and empathy can provide validation and guidance for continuing to overcome. Having the support of others will aid us in gaining new perspectives, challenging self-limiting beliefs, and providing the encouragement and support we need to continue the journey of rewriting our narrative. I am healed, and now that I am home, I am taking steps to build a stronger support system so that I can continue rewriting the narrative and remain emotionally healthy as I move forward in life. My friends, having Jesus and a therapist or coach is okay. You got Jesus and a medical doctor.

In closing, rewriting the narrative after healing from emotional injuries is a life-changing process that empowers us to reclaim what the devil stole from us. We can reclaim our lives and reshape our self-perception and perception of God. It involves acknowledging God's truth, our pain, reframing our beliefs about God, ourselves, and our experiences, and cultivating new practices (spiritual and self-care), and seeking support as we remain focused and know who we are. By embracing our resilience and growth, we can create a new narrative that reflects God's Word, our strength, worthiness, and capacity for healing. This process allows us to move forward with a renewed sense of purpose, perspective, self-compassion, resilience, and transformation amidst adversity. We gain a deep appreciation for the power we have gained through our healing journey, which permits us to reclaim our identity, cultivate compassion, and discover new depths of wisdom and purpose. By tapping into the power within us, we can navigate the challenges with grace, create a narrative that aligns with our inner truth, and move forward with hope and renewed strength.

Scriptures of Strength

2 Corinthians 12:9-10 1 Corinthians 16:13

Psalms 22:19 Psalms 28:7-8

CHAPTER EIGHT

REFINE

"My mission in life is not merely to survive but to thrive and to do so with some passion, some compassion, some humor, and some style." – Maya Angelou

Our ability to refine our lives after healing from emotional pain and damage is a testament to the power of God and the resilience of the human spirit when connected to God. When we embark on the path to healing, we gain valuable insights and wisdom that allow us to intentionally shape our lives to align with our authentic selves and values. We are no longer defined by our circumstances and pain but refined by the things we experience. Through healing, we can redefine our priorities, develop healthy boundaries, and cultivate a more profound sense of self-awareness. This allows us to build and maintain healthy relationships and show up differently as we navigate life.

As we heal from emotional injuries, we become more attuned to our needs, desires, and aspirations. This heightened self-awareness empowers us to make conscious choices and take intentional actions that support our well-being and personal growth. We may seek new experiences, relationships, or opportunities aligning with our newfound clarity and understanding. Refining our lives creates space for joy, fulfillment, and meaningful connections. We can redefine our relationships, career paths, and personal goals, allowing us to live more authentically and purposefully.

Refining our lives after healing from emotional pain is not always linear or without challenges, but it offers the potential for reflective growth and transformation. I can admit that the things I have learned in this GAP season, I don't believe I would have gained any other way. God allowed it for a reason. I must continue nurturing my spiritual and emotional well-being, practicing self-care, and surrounding myself with positive influences. I encourage you to do the same. By doing so, we can continue to refine our lives and create a future grounded in healing, resilience, and a deep sense of self-empowerment. My friends refining our lives requires ongoing spiritual growth, personal development, self-reflection, self-compassion, and a willingness to embrace change. It also requires us to use the right weapons to fight the battle of spiritual warfare and tap into the transformative power of divine love and compassion.

SPIRITUAL WEAPONS

The weapons of our warfare are not physical [weapons of flesh and blood]. Our weapons are divinely powerful for the destruction of fortresses – 2 Corinthians 10:4 (AMP).

Our weapons are reading God's Word, meditation on God's Word, memorizing Scripture, singing, praise and worship, and prayer. We must practice using them daily to refine our proficiency, for when the battle heats up, we are familiar with what to do with them and which one to use at a particular time. We must practice them daily to develop and strengthen our spiritual muscles.

- Reading the Word: to become aware of what God expects of us.

- Meditation: To gain knowledge and understanding of what was read and how to apply it practically to our lives and circumstances.

- Memorizing: It is a part of meditation. It allows us to hide the Word in our hearts because we may not always have a Bible when the enemy attacks or when sharing God's Truth with someone else.

- Singing: Releases the Word from our lips. This is usually associated with praise and worship.

- Praise and worship: Giving honor and glory to God.

- Prayer: Communication with God. This should be done in spirit and in truth.

- Fasting: Spiritual discipline of abstaining from all or some kinds of food or drink.

Friends, we must practice using our weapons daily. We use them when things are going well and when the trials of life come to test our faith. We build confidence by using our spiritual weapons as we spend time with Jesus. Faith is built before the fight, not a by-product of the fight. Just as athletes train daily for hours to prepare to perform, so must we as Christians train many hours in preparation for when trouble knocks at the door of our lives. Hardships will come. The adversary will try to use them to his advantage. The question is, will you be ready to face them and properly use your spiritual weapons to maintain joy and peace as you fight to overcome them victoriously? Victory is possible with the right trainer (Jesus) and diet (Word of God). We cannot keep a worldly diet, insert Jesus here and there, and expect miracle-working power during the heat of the battle. We can't have part-time faith and expect full-time victory. No sir and no ma'am, it does not work that way. I will repeat it; what you put in is what you get out. How you practice is how you will fight.

I encourage you to designate at least 30 minutes daily with God in His Word. It is imperative that we have that one-on-one to cultivate a genuine relationship with our Lord. Fellowship is necessary. We must also place on the: full armor of God. It is not optional but vital for our protection and victory. Read Ephesians 6: 12-18. Fasting can aid in breaking strongholds, releasing emotional burdens, and fostering a renewed sense of inner peace and restoration on the healing path.

POWER OF DIVINE LOVE AND COMPASSION

"Now to Him who is able to do exceedingly abundantly above all we ask or think, according to the power that works in us" – Ephesians 3:20.

My husband and I repeat this verse almost daily in our prayers. We have come to understand the power that works in us. This power is transformative. It provides the encouragement we need to endure daily and overcome past strife and current circumstances that have detained us for so long. We are intentional with tapping into that power daily.

Tapping into the transformative power of divine love and compassion has been my husband's and I's saving grace during this GAP season. The power within us brings reflective and comprehensive benefits that have enhanced our overall well-being. It fosters inner healing and emotional well-being that we cannot receive from external things. It acts as a healing balm, soothing our emotional wounds and allowing us to release pain, resentment, unforgiveness, and fear. It brings comfort, peace, and a sense of wholeness, promoting inner harmony and resilience in the face of life's challenges and woes.

Secondly, our ability to tap into divine love and compassion expands our capacity for empathy and connections. It opens our hearts to the struggle and joys of others, fostering a genuine sense of understanding and compassion. This enhanced empathy allows for more meaningful and authentic relationships, enabling a sense of belonging and mutual support. It also encourages us to extend kindness and compassion to others, creating a positive ripple effect in communities and contributing to a more harmonious and compassionate society. Having a culture of people that are more than willing to extend grace through forgiveness and lending second chances to those who make mistakes instead of holding the mistakes over their heads, defining them by those mistakes, and keeping them from true forward movement.

Lastly, the transformative power of divine love and compassion facilitates personal growth and self-transformation. By embracing this power, we recognize our inherent worthiness and true potential. It empowers us to let go of self-limiting and self-destructive beliefs and adopt a mindset of self-acceptance, self-love, and forgiveness. We gain l.o.v.e. (liberty of vulnerable emotions). This transformation opens the door to personal growth, resilience, and realizing our divine purpose, leading to a more fulfilling and purpose-driven life. A life of more than survival but thriving.

BEING INTENTIONAL

Connecting to the transformative power of divine love and compassion is a daily feat, and it requires us to be conscious and intentional in our approach. Here are a few ways I nurture a connection with this power daily:

1. Spiritual practice: I engage in daily spiritual practices such as prayer, meditation, Scripture memorization, praise, and worship. These practices allow me to have a deeper awareness of God's divine presence within and around me.

2. Study habits: I read and study God's Word daily to renew my mind. I seek to practically apply the Word to all situations and interactions with people. One way of making the Word applicable is by studying the life of Jesus and how He demonstrated love and compassion.

3. Self-Compassion: Learning to extend grace to me and forgive me. The extension of divine love and compassion to self must be practiced. I have learned to be gentle with myself, recognizing that I am a child of God who loved me so much that He sent His Only Begotten Son to die for me. Therefore, I released self-judgment and

past mistakes and offered complete forgiveness to myself. Doing so has cultivated a foundation for extending love and compassion to myself and others.

4. Serve others: Engaging in acts of love, kindness, and services and seeking opportunities to alleviate the sufferings of others aids me in not elevating my problems and circumstance. By extending love to those around me who are in need, I can be transformed by the power of divine love. I can be light in the darkness. Love in an environment that thrived on hate.

5. Sense of gratitude: I cultivated an attitude of gratitude, acknowledging the blessings and goodness in my life. By focusing on the positive aspects and expressing gratitude by writing down at least three things I am grateful for daily, my heart is open to receiving and sharing divine love and compassion. My friends, gratitude shifts our perspective and helps us recognize the holy presence of God in every situation or circumstance.

My friends, remember that tapping into the transformative power of divine love and compassion is an ongoing practice. It requires intentionality, patience, and a willingness to surrender to God's divine order and authority. Embrace the journey with an open heart and a commitment to live from a place of love and compassion, embodied with peace. Such willingness will transform your life and the lives of those around you.

STRATEGIES FOR GAINING POWER

The healing process is a transformative journey that requires inner strength and empowerment that can only be obtained from God. Gaining power during the fight is crucial as it allows us to reclaim our sense of self, rebuild our resilience, and navigate the challenges that arise. Accessing divine power will enable us to land a powerful left hook – providing a profound source of strength and guidance from the Holy Spirit. By recognizing our connection to God, we tap into a wellspring of wisdom, love, and support that can assist us in our healing and recovery.

Implementing strategies for gaining power during the healing process involves several key elements.

Self-awareness and self-compassion. This requires us to acknowledge our emotions, thoughts, and experiences without judgment; we create space for healing and growth. I suggest meditation, prayer, and journaling to deepen your self-awareness and connection with the divine within you.

Setting boundaries. We must prioritize our well-being and establish healthy spiritual and personal boundaries in relationships and activities that may hinder our progress.

Self-care. Taking time to rest, relax and engage in activities that bring us joy, nourishment, and peace rejuvenates our spirit and strengthens our resolve.

Support. Seeking support and guidance from spiritual mentors/coaches, therapists, or support groups can provide valuable insights and encouragement along the healing process. Our support system should offer guidance, wisdom, and a compassionate presence that helps us traverse the complexities of healing.

ACTIVATING THE POWER

Activating the power within is imperative. The Scriptures remind us that we are fearfully and wonderfully made. We are created in the image of a loving and powerful God. We are endowed with divine potential and purpose. By tapping into the power within, we align ourselves with God's plan for our lives and unleash our true potential.

The Bible encourages us to have faith, reminding us that all things are possible with God. We also know that all things work together for the good of those who love God and are called according to

His purpose. When we activate the power within us through faith, we recognize that we are not alone in our journey. A Sovereign God supports us. He who has all-power and who equips us with strength, wisdom, and guidance. We can draw upon His promises, such as "I can do all things through Christ who strengthens me" (Philippians 4:13) or "No weapon formed against me shall prosper and every tongue which rises against me in judgment I shall condemn" (Isaiah 54:17, personalized). Such promises and more aid in overcoming obstacles and pursuing our hopes and dreams with unwavering determination.

Activating the power within us instills a sense of purpose and divine calling. We are reminded that our talents and gifts are meant to be used for the glory of God and the betterment of others. By embracing our unique abilities and activating them in service to God and humanity, we experience fulfillment and a deep sense of meaning. Scripture encourages us to "shine our light before others" (Matthew 5:15), reminding us that our actions and accomplishments can inspire and positively impact those around us. With the power of God within us, we are motivated to live a life of purpose, impact, and eternal significance. Friends, please don't let the enemy use your painful circumstances against you. He desires to drain you of your power and knock you to the canvas of life. The devil seeks to rob you of your destiny. Remember, tapping into the transformative power of divine love and compassion opens the door to numerous benefits that positively impact our well-being and how we relate to God, ourselves, others, and the world around us. Get up and start throwing those jabs. You still have plenty of fight in you and life to live. God has a plan, even if you do not understand His will. Just keep powering through.

When we combine practical strategies with a spiritual perspective, we tap into a wellspring of divine power that empowers us during the healing process. This integration allows us to draw strength from God, finding meaning in our experiences even when we do not understand why God allowed them, and experience the transformation that the power of unwavering faith, divine love, and speaking the redemptive names of the Lord can bring as we continue the journey towards healing and recovery. Do not stop throwing those jabs, crosses, and powerful hook combinations. Power up!

Scriptures of Strength

Nehemiah 8:10 Habakkuk 3:19

Exodus 15:2 1 Chronicles 16:11

CHAPTER NINE

RELEASE

I am a firm believer in the fact that there is absolutely no limit to what God can and will do in and through our situations (good or bad). That is, one, we allow; two, we separate ourselves from sin; and three, we choose to be an instrument for His use. When we allow God to be in our lives in every aspect, we learn the actual value of love and faith. I know this and believe and live it. After having my "come to Jesus" meeting in this GAP season, I am very intentional about inviting Abba into every aspect of my life – every situation, good or bad. I intentionally verbalize that I choose to take up my cross and follow my Lord and Savior, Big Brother Jesus Christ, daily. I choose to live a life of love. I am intentional about growing and sharing love. Why?

Faith worketh through love – Galatians 5:6b

Faith is birth out of love. Love is a command that comes from our Father, who is in heaven. We must acknowledge and accept our duty to love to talk about faith. Love is necessary for our ability to have faith, develop, practice, and demonstrate faith. We can thrive in a world filled with hate and selfishness.

POWER RELEASE

Much like our cell phones must be connected to a charger to power up, we as believers must remain connected to our power source for faith to flow full force in our lives. Our knowing, agreement, and dependence determine the power flow and pressure. Trust in God's

Word can turn trials into virtual classrooms for spiritual growth. Endurance, fortitude, and integrity – God wants us to mature as His children and bear much good fruit for the kingdom. Total dependence on God will also provide us with what we need to conquer the spirits of rejection, fear, shame, and hopelessness. To dig up damaged roots of pain and fear and allow the fruit of the Spirit to take root within us. Total dependence on God will provide us with the means to overcome anything that bounds us mentally and emotionally to our past or keeps us from complete surrender to God in our present. Dependence on God will yield the power to heal emotional injuries contributing to damaged or untrained souls.

Do you remember me mentioning free will and us needing to be good stewards of the gift? When we do not use free will wisely, God will often allow us to work (choose) ourselves into a position from which only He can deliver us. In those moments, He will break us to reshape and mend all our brokenness. He then chooses the correct and exact instrument (trial, predicament, hardship, lack, etc.) He needs to refine us. Sometimes the tools are pointed and sharp. Pain and suffering may accompany them, but He knows exactly how much we can take without breaking our spirit. He wants us to correct course. He is after our stubborn self-will. His sole purpose is to drive out whatever keeps us from being in full fellowship and relationship with Him. Whatever or whoever hinders our relationship with Him must be removed.

Believe it or not, my friends, we grow when the odds are against us. We must stand in faith and draw near to God and depend on Him for the victory to be ours. By drawing near to God, I have allowed Him to work His will in my heart. That is why hope increased, and I remained closed in my right mind as I sat in the cold, unforgiving cell awaiting trial and believing for deliverance. That is why I could dream. I could plan for a future with my husband and children and make faith moves. I have learned that faith does not eliminate problems but makes them more manageable to endure. Faith makes things possible.

My friends, knowing, agreeing, and depending on God is a lifelong process. Practicing faith is a daily choice. Our choice is to be intentional daily to engage in the process and grow. Life is choice driven. The internal, unseen essentials should be our primary focus in life – faith. We must connect, know, agree, and depend on God so that the power of faith can be released to help us on this journey called life. Especially when turbulent winds, heavy rain, and hail hit our lives. When the earthquake rocks our world and threatens to split it apart, faith can cause it to mend after we endure. Faith also allows us to stand as we endure. We need faith to level up and overcome the wiles of the enemy and the things in life he uses to gain access to our thoughts.

We need faith to connect to God through Christ so we can fight with the right weapons and fight the right enemy. The fight is in the spirit realm. Also, remember, a faith not tested is faith that cannot be trusted. So, see your problems, troubles, etc., as a test. Strong faith can be anyone's when things are good. What kind of faith do you have when things are upside down and twisted from the storms of life ripping your world apart? Faith is the key to leveling up over it all.

FAITH

Faith is a fact. Faith is an action. One definition of faith that I have heard and often repeat is "Faith is believing that God is telling the truth and acting like it." Faith is vital to our Christian walk. I hear you quoiting Hebrews 11:1, "Now faith is the substance of things hoped for, the evidence of things not seen" (KJV). I used to quote this Scripture all the time. I lacked knowledge and proper understanding of the power within it.

I have identified three levels of faith that I have, and they keep me off the ropes and out of the corner when life throws mighty blows. These levels of faith also aides me in handling challenging situations with the proper perspective.

Now Faith. Remember, Hebrews 11:1 states, "Now faith is…" Now faith is necessary for having the ability to power up during major and minor storms. Now faith is present. Now faith requires action. It requires that we act as if God is telling the truth by applying His Word as the moment to whatever situation we are dealing with. Now Faith gives us the confidence to walk without heads held high and to press forward with the confidence of God. Knowing that in due time His promises will manifest in our situation.

Now faith prompts us to make faith moves. My husband and I have made many faith moves in this GAP season. The writing of this book is one. I believed God would restore my physical freedom, so I worked to be prepared to receive it. I was given a vision, and I wrote it down. Now faith gives me the strength to keep moving forward with hope. The power enables us to trust God for greater, even though what we see states the opposite.

Strong Faith. Faith, in general, is developed before the battle and is tested in the fight. I believe applying God's Word to our situations enhances the strength of faith. When we continue to surrender the problem to God and pour His Word into us, we allow faith to grow. The more we apply faith, the more it grows in strength. Faith comes by hearing and hearing by the Word of God – Romans 10:17. Faith is developed through listening to the Word taught, preached, and discussed. I have found that the more I share God's truth with others during this season, the more strength I acquire. Every conversation becomes focused on God's Word, which releases power for me to keep pressing forward.

> *"For whatever is born of God overcomes the world. And*
> *this is the victory that has overcome the world, our faith"*
> *– 1 John 5:4-5.*

Friends, if the Word of God is not in us when the trials of life come, we will not have what it takes to overcome and be victorious.

Long faith. This form of faith is developed as we endure fights that are prolonged. When there is a delay in deliverance. Long faith determines or tests our faithfulness in God. Do we really trust Him? Will we continue to trust Him even when things are not going as planned or hoped for? Will we continue to praise, worship, and pray, even when He is not sending the rescue squad?

Accepting God's timing has developed my long faith. By surrendering my desires and timeline and trusting in His divine wisdom, I gain the fortitude to hold on a bit longer. Friends, in the surrender, we find liberation from the pressures of our own timelines and expectations. By embracing God's timing, we open ourselves to His perfect plan, knowing that His ways are higher than our own and that His timing is always purposeful and impeccable.

I have learned that God wants our faith to be developed. He wants us to grow in our relationship and fellowship with Him. To be better acquainted with Jesus. He will allow us to stay in certain situations to grow us. We must take heed of the training and allow Him to work. Listen, although I made poor choices that got me in this mess of a situation, through my total surrender, God has used it to develop me. For years I wondered why God did not arrange for my release. Why was there a lack of progression in the case? Why was I still stagnant? Why did everyone around me seem to be getting their cases resolved and moving forward, and I was still sitting behind the cold, unforgiving walls? The lyrics "He's preparing me for greater" came to mind. Reminding me that God is working a miracle just for me, and it will be BIG! During my lengthy detainment, I received the revelation that character-building, and refinement were taking place. Healing was in progress, and I had to allow God to have His way.

Listen to me, do not allow the enemy to trick you out of your faith. Faith is available to all, regardless of your current situation, positioning, or past. No matter how many mistakes, poor choices, or sinful things you have done, it is faith that God honors. If we seek forgiveness and repent – turn away from sinful living, toxic thinking patterns, and worldly theology, God is faithful to restore our broken lives. He is not a respecter of person. He gives us all a measure of faith. It is up to us if we develop it and use it.

Do you remember the story of Rehab? She is in the lineage of Jesus. Rehab was a prostitute. However, because of her faith, she was honored by God. Much like Rehab, I have a tainted background, but I refuse to allow it to determine my faith in God. I know He is a forgiving God. He is my Redeemer. Therefore, I know all hope is not lost. I can still be used for the edification of His kingdom. This book is proof. My faith is strong, long, and now. I encourage you to release the power of faith by being obedient to what God has told you to do. That is what I did and continue to do. Just because your background is stained does not mean you cannot have the faith experience and a life of abundance.

> *"I, the LORD invite you to come and talk it over. Your sins are scarlet red, but they will be whiter than snow or wool" – Isaiah 1:18 (CEV).*

If you believe your background will keep you from moving forward with God, then you do not entirely understand the value of faith. God wants you to believe Him. To trust that what He has said to you is true. To stand on that truth. If you want God to protect you from the fire as He did for Rehab and her household, make the decision to trust Him and, through obedience, stand firm on that belief. God moves according to our faith and not our education, experience, explanations, or excuses. Step out of the corner, get off the ropes, and rise from the canvas by releasing that left hook of faith.

PRACTICE FAITH

Through this GAP, I learned many lessons. The most impactful and transformative lesson has been that of practicing faith. I have learned to trust God in all things and with all things. That includes the good, bad, ugly, pretty, uncomfortable, unlovely, undesirable, and painful. Those things I lack understanding and wisdom, I turn them all over to Jesus and don't worry about them. Each lesson taught me to relinquish my pride, fear, pain, and more as I grabbed hold of the truth God was telling and showing me. Yes, I said it, I, Dr. Daniels, let go of pride. That is the number one reason many stay stuck in mess because of haughty attitudes and lack of humility (false humility). God has shown me He and pride cannot reside in the same heart. I had to make a choice. In my Jeopardy contestant's voice, "I choose God for five thousand Alex."

This brings me to the steps I developed to help me practice releasing faith in all situations – minor or major. I pray it will bless you and allow you to release faith at all cost. Remember, how you practice is how you will perform. So, when the pop quiz comes, try to practice well. The test may be around the corner. You must be intentional.

Faith Practice Steps:

1. Stop – James 1:19 should occur – slow to speak, quick to listen, slow to anger.

2. Think – identify feelings and think about how to apply God's Word at the moment despite your feelings. Put away pride and humble self.

3. Acknowledge – God's truth and the prompting of the Holy Spirit.

4. Respond – with loving words and actions.

I use This STAR method with clients and clearly now in my own life. Who doesn't want to be a star? To shine in the midst of darkness. I did, and I do! When an offense occurs, do the following:

1. Pray for the person the enemy used as a tool to attack me.

2. Pray God's Word and promises back to Him.

3. Ask for help with overcoming any lingering (-) (strong) thoughts and/or feelings.

4. Ask for wisdom in areas where I lack understanding or how to respond differently if I fail to do so in love.

5. Ask God for wisdom regarding the lesson(s) He wanted me to learn, skills, or spirit He is trying to develop in me.

Remember, faith is our trust in God. We develop that trust as we learn to fellowship with Him and grow in our relationship with Him. We learn to understand and depend on Him more. Honor and worship Him in our lives. My favorite passage of Scripture,

Trust in the Lord with all your heart; lean not to your own understanding. In all your ways acknowledge Him, and He will direct your path – Proverbs 3:5-6.

We can replace the word trust with faith to see the action of faith as it takes root in our lives. Faith moves us beyond what we cannot see. It allows us to enter the spirit realm where God operates. We can connect with His super while we are in the natural, and it brings forth His supernatural power to aid us. Come on, Jesus! My friends, faith keeps us in alignment with God. It is necessary for forward movement and for us to rise above adversity.

There is a saying, "Practice makes perfect." This may be true, but we must recognize that what we practice and how we practice may be detrimental to our performance or success. When I first began to play basketball, I would shoot my free throws by standing on the left side of the free-throw line. I was making my free throws, but my form needed to be corrected. One of my father's friends took me to the gym and had me practice shooting free throws from the middle of the line. When we practice faith, we must ensure that our form is correct. That we have faith in God and we are obedient to His Word.

LOVE

I can only talk about faith by acknowledging and accepting my duty to love. Faith is birth out of love (see Galatians 5:6). Love is essential to our ability to develop, practice, and live by faith. Love becomes active through knowledge of God's Word.

In my God-allowed pause, I have become better acquainted with Love. God is love, according to 1 John 4:8. In understanding that God is the very nature of what I must express when facing trials, tribulations, suffering, and situations, I am better equipped to handle, deal with, and endure without being consumed. I understand that love is an action (1 John 3:18). Love is the power charge that prompts me to handle people with care (John 15:12-13). Love has become my primary value and how I show up each day. I view life through the lens of love. I have chosen to live a life of love. Love is a lifestyle that I have cultivated and work each day to maintain.

In my efforts to cultivate and maintain a love lifestyle, I had to truly understand the power of Love and all He does in my life. I will share a few things that help me to level up in my current situation.

Love purchased me – Christ gave His life to purchase me, save me from every sin, and redeem me from mistakes, situations, and predicaments. The things that stand in my way of joy, peace, and a life of abundance, He has won the victory over the enemy for me. He has eradicated the curse.

"He was wounded for my transgressions. He was bruised for my iniquities. The chastisement of my peace was upon Him, and by His stripes, I am healed" – Isaiah 53:5 (personalized).

Christ did all the work on the cross to give us the ability to rise above anything and everything that is not of Him or our Father. Christ has paid the price for my sins and yours. Also, because He paid for me, I am worthy, and no one or nothing can diminish my value. Now that

I clearly understand the root of my worth, I will live by it until I am called to eternal life.

I have been face to face with situations designed to make me feel less than in this criminal justice system and life in general. With each test, I remember who I belong to, and my true value is rooted in the purchase price Christ has already paid. When words are spoken by officers, strangers, and those in society that are meant to make me feel low, that is intended to tear me down or degrade me, I remember who I belong to.

Love liberated me.

> *"If you abide in My word, you are My disciples indeed. And you shall know the truth, and the truth shall make you free... Therefore, if the Son makes you free you shall be free indeed" – John 8: 31-32, 36.*

I have learned to place Truth (God's Word) in place of my feelings, understanding, and perception. By doing so, I have l.o.v.e. –liberty over vulnerable emotions that cause me to be spiritually blind and deaf. Love gave me new sight and clear hearing. Love set me free from the pain that imprisoned me. I was made free from sin, shame, and guilt of my past mistakes, mishaps, missteps, and more. Free from depression, low self-esteem, and false confidence and identity. Love set me free from the cold and unforgiving walls that surrounded me. To know the Truth and live it will next level you.

God's Truth is what you and I need to be released from the flawed beliefs, wrong mindsets, negative attitudes, and false or misguided perceptions about life that keep us bound. The things the enemy uses to gain access to our souls. God's Truth and the application of His Truth free you and me to be transformed and live according to what He has provided for our lives. Know the Truth, be released by the Truth, live the Truth, and be leveled up by the Truth.

DEVELOP LOVE

At new birth, when God gave us a new heart and spirit, we were given the ability to love like Him. He went so far as to provide us with His Spirit to abide within us. We have what it takes to love like Jesus, but we must grow that love. How do we grow love? We cultivate love through our obedience to God's Word. We must read it, learn it, and apply it. We make it the first and final authority in our lives. As we grow in obedience, we grow in love. Love means we do what God tells us – 2 John 6.

> *"...God has given us the Holy Spirit, who fills our hearts with His love" – Romans 5:56 (CEV).*

THE LOVE DEVELOPMENT PLAN

The ABCs of Growing Love

• A- acknowledge your ability to love and accept it – Romans 5:5

• B- Believe that everyone who loves is born of God and knows God – 1 John 4:7.

• C – confess the love of God – 1 Corinthians 13:4-8.

• D – demonstrate love in your actions, speech, and thinking – 1 John 4:12

As we develop love, we acquire a love mindset. We begin to think, speak, and act from a love perspective. I read something somewhere that stayed with me. It stated, "A step out of love is a step into trouble." A lack of obedience leads us into trouble. Maintaining a love mindset, we remain in alignment with God's will. We can faithfully and consistently apply 1 Corinthians 13: 4-8 to our daily interactions with others.

RELEASE LOVE

Love is released as we walk the love walk. In a Bible study that I taught, one assignment I gave encouraged the ladies to identify the 59 One Another's in the New Testament. I wanted to build upon their knowledge of what true love should look like. How we should interact with one another to give and receive biblical love. Some of the ones we focused on included: Build one another up (1 Thessalonians 5:11), Pray for one another (James 5:16), Live in harmony with one another (Romans 12:16), Forgive one another (Ephesians 4:32), and Love one another (Romans 12:10). Love is released when we live according to the teachings of Jesus. When we are genuinely intentional about loving our neighbor as we love ourselves. Love is released when we turn from sin and allow love to rule.

Friends, even in the most difficult, traumatic, uncomfortable situations, we must choose to love. Love is a choice. Life is choice driven. Choosing to pour love into a challenging situation is not always easy because it may go against what our feelings, emotions, senses, or even family, friends, and society are telling us. We must trust in that moment that God's Word is true. He will not lead us astray, but our feelings, emotions, senses, and other people may.

I needed a proper understanding of real love. I had to allow the Holy Spirit to teach me about biblical love. How to give and receive this love appropriately. I encourage you to let God's Spirit teach you how to love. To show you the way to surrender your heart. To love when things go wrong. To love when an offense occurs. To be patient and kind when the children are out of line. To overlook the spiteful words of another angry, bitter, and broken person. To lay gossip aside and take up words of love and grace instead. To forgive even if you believe the person does not deserve forgiveness.

I decided to remove every obstacle that would keep God's love from fully and freely flowing into the lives of others through me. Put behind resentment and unforgiveness all who had done wrong to me. Doing so caused a surge in power to increase and excel and overflow. I received what I needed to not only level up over my circumstances but to be an example of God's love even in a dark, uncomfortable, unforgiving environment. By loving as Jesus loves, I can deliver a forceful blow to K.O., the enemy. You can do the same.

PUT LOVE TO WORK

Love is the most extraordinary power we possess, capable of going beyond boundaries and overcoming the most formidable challenges. It truly never fails. When we embrace love fully and release its boundless energy, we tap into a wellspring of healing, resilience, and emotional stability. Love has the potential to create a deep sense of connection, empathy, and understanding, allowing us to navigate the complexities of life with grace and resilience. By embracing love as an active and intentional force, we unlock its immense potential to heal wounds, mend relationships, and foster emotional well-being. Through acts of kindness, compassion, and genuine care for ourselves and others, we tap into love's boundless energy, creating a ripple effect that can transform lives and bring about positive change. When channeled purposefully, love becomes a catalyst for personal growth, inner peace, and harmonious existence. Let us recognize and honor the power of love, allowing it to permeate our lives, and in doing so, we can experience the profound healing and emotional stability that it has to offer.

Don't Slip

There are many principles of faith and love. No matter how long you have been practicing these principles, you can easily slip into unbelief about the promises of God when the blows of life get too heavy and painful. We must avoid suspicion about God's promises at all cost. We do this according to Hebrews 4:11,

> *"Let us labour therefore to enter into the rest, lest any man fall after the same example of unbelief"* (KJV).

The previous verse instructs believers to follow the command to rest. We must learn to enter God's rest in times of suffering and testing. We must labor in these times. Labor means spending time in God's Word, which will stifle unbelief and any distraction. Holding tight to the promises of God by faith day after day provides the power to level up over circumstances and send the enemy running.

THERE IS POWER IN HIS NAME

During this GAP season, I learned a critical fight strategy. Speaking the redemptive name of the Lord holds immense significance in gaining strength during the fight - overcoming adversity and renewing my mind as my faith grows stronger. The name of the Lord has deep significance and power. It reminds you and me of His character, His promises, and His faithfulness. Each time I speak His name out loud or in prayer, I invite His presence into my circumstance, allowing His grace and mercy to work in my situation and life. I have called upon Jehovah Jireh-my Provider. Jehovah Rapha-my Healer, Jehovah Shalom-my Peace, and He has been present in each aspect of His character. No matter if we are calling on Jehovah Nissi-our Victory, or Jehovah Ra-ah-our Shepherd, speaking these redemptive names of the Lord, shifts our perspective from the challenges and problems before us to the unlimited power and love of our Heavenly Father.

Each time I speak one or all the redemptive names of the Lord, I affirm my trust in His sovereignty and acknowledge that He is bigger than the problem I face. It strengthens my faith, reminding me that God is with me and guiding and sustaining me through this difficult season. Each time I repeat the names of the Lord, I surrender my life and place it in His hands. Giving Him complete control, and I receive His comfort and guidance, allowing His Truth to reign and replace any thoughts that are not in alignment with His plan and purpose. My friends, I am a living witness that the redemptive names of the Lord have the power to transform our perspective, renew our minds, and provide the strength we need to press forward. I encourage you to speak His names boldly, for they are a powerful force and source of hope, encouragement, and divine intervention in times of trouble.

In speaking the redemptive names of the Lord and having an unwavering belief that He will fulfill His promises, resides an extraordinary power that transcends our human reasoning and understanding. When we declare the redemptive names of the Lord with conviction, we tap into a divine force that can move mountains, heal brokenness, manifest promises, and bring forth miraculous transformation. Through faith, we align ourselves with the infinite power of God, confidently declaring that He is faithful and able to perform everything He said He will do.

My dear friends, in the face of adversity and emotional damage, let us unleash the power of faith and love by speaking the redemptive names of the Lord. As we declare the names of Jesus, the demons tremble, for His name carries the authority to break every chain and dispel darkness. With every proclamation of Jehovah Nissi-the Lord our banner, we rise above the enemy's tactics, enveloped in the love and strength of our Heavenly Father, and reclaim our lives with unwavering faith.

STANDING FIRM ON GOD'S PROMISES

The power of standing on the promises of God in troubled times is immeasurable. When we anchor our faith in God's unchanging Word, we find hope, strength, and guidance to navigate life's challenges. His promises provide a solid foundation, assuring us of His presence, love, and faithfulness even in the midst of adversity. By trusting in His promises, we tap into a source of supernatural peace, comfort, and resilience, enabling us to face trials with courage, perseverance, and unwavering confidence. As we stand on God's promises, we experience His transformative power, witnessing firsthand how He brings beauty out of ashes and turns our trials into testimonies of His grace and redemption.

Friends, these are the promises I found and stand firm on during this GAP season. God's Word is filled with over 8,000 promises that God made to humankind. I encourage you to do as I did and search the Word for the promises that apply to you in your season of disruption, discomfort, and despair. God has already spoken to your situation. Find out what He has said and stand firm on it. Speak it, declare it, claim it, and then allow it to level you up. By doing so, you render mighty blows to the enemy of your soul.

John 3:16 For God so loved me that He gave His only begotten Son, that because I believe in Him I will not perish but have everlasting life (personalized).

1 John 5:4 Because everyone who is born from God defeats the world. And this is the victory that has defeated the world: our faith (CEB).

1 John 4:4 You, dear children, are from God and have overcome them because the one who is in you is greater than the one who is in the world (NIV).

Romans 8:28 And we know that in all things God works for the good of those who love Him, to those who are called according to His purpose (NKJV).

John 15:7 If you remain in me and my words remain in you, ask whatever you wish, and it will be done for you (NIV).

Mark 11:24 Therefore, I say to you, whatever things you ask when you pray, believe that you receive them, and you will have them (NKJV).

Philippians 1:28 Be brave when you face enemies. Your courage will show them that they are going to be destroyed, and it will show you that you will be saved. God will make all this happen (CEV).

Mark 10:27   But Jesus looked at them and said, "With men it is impossible, but not with God; for with God all things are possible" (NKJV).

Luke 1:37 For with God nothing will be impossible (NKJV).

Psalm 146:7   Who executes justice for the oppressed, who gives food to the hungry. The LORD gives freedom to the prisoners (NKJV).

Isaiah 54:17   No weapon formed against you shall prosper, and every tongue which rises against you in judgment you shall condemn…(NKJV).

Isaiah 61:1 The Spirit of the Lord God is upon Me, because the LORD has anointed Me to preach good tidings to the poor; He has sent Me to heal the brokenhearted, to proclaim liberty to the captives, and the opening of the prison to those who are bound (NKJV).

Matthew 7:7   Ask, and it will be given to you. Seek, and you will find. Knock, and the door will be opened to you (CSB).

Isaiah 56:11   So shall My word be that goes forth from My mouth; it shall not return to Me void, but it shall accomplish what I please, and it shall prosper in the things for which I sent it (NKJV).

Isiah 56:12   For you shall go out with joy and be led out with peace…(NKJV).

Scriptures of Strength

Deuteronomy 20:4   Deuteronomy 31:6

Jeremiah 32:17   Joshua 1:9

CONCLUSION

"I am thankful for my struggle because, without it, I wouldn't have stumble across my strength" – Alex Elle

Amid difficult circumstances, the journey of leveling up becomes a courageous testament to our resilience as we embrace our authentic identity, heal from emotional wounds, and experience growth and development on spiritual and personal levels. It is a path that requires unwavering determination, intentionality, and a steadfast refusal to succumb to the devil's attacks on our souls.

In the face of physical and environmental barriers within the confines of incarceration, I had to embrace the journey of healing from past and present emotional damage with the help of the Holy Spirit and the few people God sent me to aid me along this arduous but transformative path. This journey required great strength, reliance, and a solid commitment to endure. At the beginning of this fight, I did not know nor believe I possessed such an ability to overcome this blow that ended what I knew as life. However, amidst the bleakness of the cold jail walls, I learned that redemption and restoration were possible once I rekindled hope upon full surrender to God.

Overcoming the barriers and stigma of incarceration is not an easy task. The comments of judgmental people who lack knowledge of the whole truth and the limitations imposed by the judicial system can leave one feeling trapped, isolated, and lacking in many areas. However, within the depths of these constraints, with the aid of the Holy Spirit, I gained the remarkable ability to rise above adversity and seek healing.

Through a commitment to personal and spiritual growth, self-reflection, and taking advantage of stagnation, I embraced the path to healing the wounds that led to my incarceration. The journey of healing is not linear or without its challenges. Still, by fostering resilience and maintaining a hopeful outlook, one can navigate the difficult terrain and discover the strength to endure. My friends, I walked the path with limited resources and physical support. If I can do it, so can you. God will equip you if you allow Him.

Maintaining faith, love, and hope amid incarceration and difficulties is an act of defiance against circumstances that seek to weaken one's spirit and leave the soul wounded. Faith becomes a lifeline, a source of inspiration and motivation to persevere through the challenges, setbacks, and moments of despair. Faith is a power source. It provides the belief that there is a future beyond the walls of that which is consuming or detaining you.

The hope is that growth, transformation, redemption, and restoration are possible, and one's life has purpose and meaning. By cultivating faith and love, individuals can find the strength to endure the trials and tribulations of life, knowing that God does not define them by their past. He is a present help in times of trouble and a redeemer of time. My time of incarceration does not define me, but it refined me and developed me into the woman God will use for His glory.

The journey of leveling up under challenging circumstances, embracing authentic identity, healing from emotional wounds, and growing spiritually and personally is a path of empowerment and transformation. I want you to be encouraged for those who are incarcerated – mentally and physically and reading this book. Embrace the truth of God's Word and hold onto the belief that even within the confines of incarceration and the battles of life, there is the potential for transformation, redemption, and restoration. I am a living witness to what God can and will do. Keep the faith and never stop believing in the power of God. He is able and willing. Trust Him.

We must become Kingdom-focused, having a love mindset. We choose to obey the Word at all cost. Love at all cost. Faith at all cost. Be grateful at all times. Living according to these principles, we are always prepared to love up – power up during the fight. We are open to receiving from God the things necessary to next level us at any time, in any situation or season of life. Remember, this is a spiritual fight. We must operate as spiritual beings and use the right spiritual weapons to fight the opposing spirits that threaten our lives (spiritual and natural). The fight will be fought until Abba calls us home. So now is the time to gear up and fight the right enemy, having faith as our fuel and love as our foundation.

I do not profess to have all the answers. I am still in the fight, which means I am still learning. However, the things I have learned from God prompted me to share them with you. It may seem like a lot, but that is because, in this God-allowed pause, I have been through a lot and healed from numerous things. I continue to recover from my past and present. I am adamant about being who God designed me to be. That means the healthy, whole, and authentic me.

The enemy has stolen way too much from me. I am determined to take back my stuff and yours if I can. I am committed to denying satan access to my life again with God's help. Any suggestions he makes will be quickly dismissed with God's Word. I have zero energy to give to the enemy's shenanigans. I refuse to allow him to trick me out of my faith. I refuse to let him trick me out of my spot – my connection with my Divine Team. Those days are over in the Mighty name of Jesus.

I have come to the determination that my past is my past. It does not define me. I will use its lessons to continue to refine me with Christ leading me. No more people-pleasing and allowing others to determine who I am and my worth. No more compromising my values and integrity. I know who and whose I am, and nobody can change that. Anything I go through will be to enhance my character, not taint it.

I am sold out. I have given my life back to Christ. With each test I faced, I began my RAY process over. I choose to get my shine on even in the darkest moments or seasons of life. God has the final say in all situations. Therefore, I put all my faith, hope, and trust in Him. I choose to abide in His Word. I choose to walk by faith and not by sight. I choose to love. I choose Truth. I choose to be intentional – to live a life set apart for Christ. My friends, I encourage you to do the same.

I did not develop this mindset overnight. Just as all the emotional damage did not occur overnight. My healing process continues. I continue to grow spiritually and evolve personally. I am grateful. My spirit, soul, and body are connected with God's DNA flowing through me. I live for Christ. My faith is building daily as I apply God's Word practically.

Please make sure to take advantage of my next point. Faith is necessary to endure and overcome the problems we face as believers. The enemy seeks to keep us blind and deaf and ignorant of God's Truth. He uses life's ills to access our thoughts and taint beliefs. We must be alert and deny his access. Do not allow life's woes to defeat you. Allow God to use them to refine you. I am fully surrendered to God, more powerful, wiser, and better. Even in the middle of this fight, I can count it all joy, and I have the peace of God. So, I can say I am free! Praise the Lord. I'm free! No more bounds, no more chains holding me! My mind – my soul is free! After 1,438 days, God has also set me free physically as I wait for the final bell to sound. To receive the disposition of my case.

I have learned to fight the right enemy in the right environment and with the right weapons. Each time I pray for my natural enemy – I deliver a KO to the enemy of my soul! Each time I speak words of love and faith – KO! Each day I show up as my authentic self-KO to the enemy. I don't know about you, but I was born to win. No throwing in the towel. Therefore, I choose to take my rightful place as a child of God and do just that - win. He will feel the blow whenever the enemy runs up on me and hear KO. I am done living as an imposter. I am a child of God, and I own it fully. My identity is in Christ, and I receive it; that is how I choose to show up in life. Right now! Yes, even before the final disposition, I have decided to show up as she whom my Father designed.

I am H.E.R. (Healed Evolved Restored) and

S.H.E. is me (Surrendered Hopeful Encouraged)

Friends, if God allows it, He will use it for our good. Even this GAP season is working for my good. What the enemy meant for evil, God has worked it out for my good. He will do the same in your situation if you allow Him. We are doomed to repeat the same conditions and remain stuck in a vicious, toxic cycle until we understand the spiritual fight we are engaged in, who our enemy is, and how he gains access to our lives. Once we can fight the correct enemy and use the right weapons, we can overcome the things that bound us. We accept God's covering and learn to feel – deal – heal. Unaddressed offenses and unhealed emotional injuries steal from us. They take our joy and peace, steal or distort our identity and infect our thoughts and beliefs.

When healing takes place, our authentic identity is restored. We are refined in our character, and with the help of our Heavenly Team, we level up. We can operate on the next level of purpose as God's promises manifest in our lives. We see life from the eyes of love and the lens of faith. My friends, put your gloves up and keep fighting. Keep standing until the final bell sounds. That is what I am doing. I will see you around because at the sound of the final bell, the end of this GAP season, I declare that God will restore every aspect of my life. When you embrace love and faith, the past pain and everything attached to it loses its power. Love is freedom. Faith is power. It's time to level up. Stay kingdom focused! Power up, and I will see you on the other side of healing.